Language Arts Warm-Ups: Expanding Vocabulary

Authors: Cindy Barden, Ann Fisher, and Jane Heitman
Editor: Mary Dieterich
Proofreaders: April Albert and Margaret Brown

COPYRIGHT © 2016 Mark Twain Media, Inc.

ISBN 978-1-62223-590-2

Printing No. CD-404245

Mark Twain Media, Inc., Publishers
Distributed by Carson-Dellosa Publishing LLC

The purchase of this book entitles the buyer to reproduce the student pages for classroom use only. Other permissions may be obtained by writing Mark Twain Media, Inc., Publishers.

All rights reserved. Printed in the United States of America.

Visit us at www.carsondellosa.com

Table of Contents

Introduction 1

Root Words, Prefixes, and Suffixes .. 2
   Introduction to Root Words, Prefixes,
      and Suffixes 2
   Root Words, Prefixes, and Suffixes 4
   Prefixes 6
   Prefixes With Negative Meanings 8
   Prefixes Denoting Numbers 11
   Prefixes *over-* and *under-* 13
   Prefixes *in-*, *im-*, and *ex-* 13
   Prefixes Denoting Size and Position 14
   Prefix Review 16
   Suffixes 19
   Adding Suffixes 21
   Suffixes *-er*, *-or*, *-est* 22
   Suffixes *-ly* and *-ful* 23
   Suffixes *-less*, *-tion*, *-ation* 24
   Suffixes *-able* and *-ment* 25
   Suffixes *-ology*, *-ist*, *-phobia* 26
   Suffixes *-ish*, *-ness*, *-an* 27
   Suffix Review 28
   Words With Prefixes & Suffixes 30
   Root Words, Prefixes, and Suffixes
      Review 33

Compound Words 35
   Compound Words 35

Vocabulary 44
   Confusing Word Pairs 44
   Homophones 46
   Homographs 48
   Synonyms 49
   Antonyms 50
   Proper Nouns and Proper Adjectives 51
   Changing the Part of Speech of Words ... 52
   Words From Mythology 53
   Classifying Words 54
   Foreign Words and Phrases 56
   Latin Phrases 57

Figurative Language 59
   Idioms 59
   Imagery 61
   Simile 64
   Metaphor 66
   Adage 68
   Cliché 70
   Personification 72
   Allusion 74
   Symbolism 75
   Hyperbole 77
   Synecdoche 79

Dictionary Skills 80
   Using a Dictionary/Thesaurus 80

Answer Keys 81

Introduction

Language Arts Warm-Ups: Expanding Vocabulary provides students with mental warm-ups to help them prepare for the day's lesson while reviewing what they have previously learned. These short warm-up activities provide teachers and parents with a variety of ways for students to practice and reinforce their language arts skills.

Activities include a variety of formats such as multiple choice, fill-in-the-blank, short answer, concept application, and creative responses. Warm-ups in the figurative language section may also be used for story starters for their own writing. Students may need to complete some of the activities on their own paper.

Topics covered in *Language Arts Warm-Ups: Expanding Vocabulary* include root words, prefixes, and suffixes; compound words; vocabulary; and figurative language. All the activities are designed to improve students' vocabularies for better reading comprehension and writing fluency. The activities can be used in any order to best meet your teaching needs.

Each page may be copied and cut apart so that the individual sections can be used as quick warm-up activities to begin each day. The teacher may also give the student the entire page to keep in a folder or binder and complete as assigned. A transparency of the page may be made to project the activities for the whole class to see. A digital copy of the page can also be projected on the class whiteboard or projection device. Extra copies of warm-ups may also be kept in the class learning center for students to complete when they have spare time for review or when the class has a few minutes before lunch or dismissal.

The book has been correlated to current state, national, and provincial standards. Correlations for the book that apply to your location and needs may be found at www.carsondellosa.com.

Root Words, Prefixes, and Suffixes

#001. Introduction to Root Words, Prefixes, and Suffixes 1

For each **root word**, add a **suffix** and a **prefix** of your choice. Write a sentence using your new word.

1. believe
   _____
   _____

2. port
   _____
   _____

3. print
   _____
   _____

#002. Introduction to Root Words, Prefixes, and Suffixes 2

Draw lines to show which prefixes can be added to which root words. You may draw more than one line to or from each word part.

1. in   action

                regard

2. dis   assemble

                come

3. re   pay

                form

#003. Introduction to Root Words, Prefixes, and Suffixes 3

A *biweekly* meeting occurs twice a week, according to the first definition in most dictionaries. However, the second definition usually states that a biweekly event is one that occurs every two weeks. What is another way you could describe something that occurs twice a month to make it very clear?

_____
_____
_____
_____
_____

#004. Introduction to Root Words, Prefixes, and Suffixes 4

Circle all the words that are spelled correctly. Rewrite the incorrect words on the lines below.

careful   tuneing   fitted
regularly   swiming

_____
_____
_____
_____

Root Words, Prefixes, and Suffixes

#005. Introduction to Root Words, Prefixes, and Suffixes 5

Write two sentences about things you can do *amazingly* well.

1. _____
   _____
   _____

2. _____
   _____
   _____

#006. Introduction to Root Words, Prefixes, and Suffixes 6

Remove the prefix and suffix in the bold word and write it on the first line. Then write a new sentence using the root word.

Max was very **uncomfortable** in his tuxedo and dress shoes.

root word: _____

new sentence:

_____
_____
_____

#007. Introduction to Root Words, Prefixes, and Suffixes 7

Which of these contains a **root word** that means *to pinpoint the place of something*? Circle your choices, then write a sentence using one of those words on the lines below.

relocate   locomotion
locust tree   located
locatable

_____
_____
_____

#008. Introduction to Root Words, Prefixes, and Suffixes 8

Add a prefix and a suffix to *compare*. Use your new word in a sentence.

new word: _____

sentence:

_____
_____
_____

Root Words, Prefixes, and Suffixes

#009. Root Words, Prefixes, and Suffixes 1

1. A **root word** is a word that can be changed into a new word by adding a **prefix** and/or **suffix** to it. *Like* is a root word. Write two other examples of root words.
   _____

2. A prefix is added to the beginning of a word to change its meaning. (*dislike*) Write two more examples.
   _____

3. A suffix is added to the end of a word and changes its meaning. (*likely*) Write two more examples.
   _____

4. Some words can contain both a prefix and a suffix. (*unlikely*) Write two more examples.
   _____

#010. Root Words, Prefixes, and Suffixes 2

For many years, one of the longest words in some unabridged dictionaries was *antidisestablishmentarianism*. Break the word down by listing all the prefixes and suffixes in it. Find the root word, too.

Prefixes	Root Word	Suffixes

Now try to figure out its meaning. Write your guess below, then check with a large dictionary or the teacher's answer key to see if you got it right.
_____
_____

#011. Root Words, Prefixes, and Suffixes 3

Circle the words that share similar meanings. Use a dictionary if necessary. Write a sentence for one of the words below.

    antitoxin   antiphony

    antibodies   antiserum

    antidote

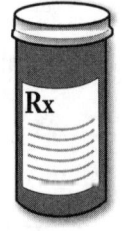

_____
_____

#012. Root Words, Prefixes, and Suffixes 4

1. The spelling of root words usually does not change when prefixes are added. Example: *sell* and *resell*. Write two more examples.
   _____
   _____

2. In the words *real, really,* and *road,* the *re-* at the beginning of the words is not a prefix. Why not?
   _____
   _____
   _____

Root Words, Prefixes, and Suffixes

#013. Root Words, Prefixes, and Suffixes 5

Write the root words.

1. **unthinkable** _____
2. **illegal** _____
3. **honesty** _____
4. **mismanagement** _____
5. **impossible** _____
6. **disconnection** _____

#014. Root Words, Prefixes, and Suffixes 6

Add a prefix, suffix, or both to each root word. Write the new words.

1. **luck** _____
2. **quick** _____
3. **sleep** _____
4. **reach** _____
5. **pay** _____
6. **read** _____

#015. Root Words, Prefixes, and Suffixes 7

Sometimes the spelling of a root word changes when a suffix is added. Write the root words. Check a dictionary if you are not sure of the spelling.

1. **unbelievable** _____
2. **unhappily** _____
3. **reappearance** _____
4. **unfriendly** _____
5. **rechargeable** _____
6. **disagreement** _____

#016. Root Words, Prefixes, and Suffixes 8

Add the prefix *re-* to each word and use it in a short sentence.

1. **move** _____
_____
2. **pay** _____
_____
3. **place** _____
_____

What do you think the prefix *re-* means?
_____
_____

Root Words, Prefixes, and Suffixes

#017. Prefixes 1

A **prefix** is added to the beginning of a word and changes its meaning. Adding a prefix sometimes changes the spelling of the **root word**.

The prefixes **un-** and **non-** mean **not**. Add the prefix **un-** or **non-** to each word to create a new word. Write a brief definition for each new word. Use a dictionary to check spelling and definitions.

1. **likely** _____
2. **profit** _____
3. **sense** _____
4. **tidy** _____

#018. Prefixes 2

The prefixes **in-**, **il-**, **ir-**, and **im-** all mean **not**. Create new words by adding one of those prefixes to these words. Write a brief definition for each new word. Use a dictionary to check spelling and definitions.

1. **logical** _____
2. **mature** _____
3. **active** _____
4. **literate** _____
5. **regular** _____

#019. Prefixes 3

Circle "T" for true or "F" for false. Use a dictionary to check your answers.

1. T F **Prefixes** can completely change the meaning of words.
2. T F *Hyperactive* and *hypoactive* have opposite meanings.
3. T F **Prefixes** are added to the beginning of a word.
4. T F The spelling of a **root word** may change when prefixes are added.

#020. Prefixes 4

Pre- means **before**; **post-** means **after**; **dis-** means to do the **opposite**; and **re-** means **to do again**. Match the words with their definitions.

___ 1. **preseason**   A. doubt
___ 2. **distrust**   B. after earning a degree
___ 3. **postgraduate**   C. before the regular season
___ 4. **regroup**   D. change around

Language Arts Warm-Ups: Expanding Vocabulary   Root Words, Prefixes, and Suffixes

Name: _____ Date: _____

Root Words, Prefixes, and Suffixes

#021. Prefixes 5

Answer the following questions on the lines below.

1. How can knowing the meaning of a **prefix** help us figure out the meaning of a new word?

   _____
   _____

2. Use a dictionary to explain the difference in meaning between *interstate* and *intrastate*.

   _____
   _____
   _____

#022. Prefixes 6

Trans- means **across**, *inter-* means **between**, and *sub-* means **below**. Use a dictionary to write three or more words that begin with each prefix.

1. *trans-* _____
   _____

2. *inter-* _____
   _____

3. *sub-* _____
   _____

#023. Prefixes 7

Circle "T" for true or "F" for false. Use a dictionary to check your answers.

1. T F *Inflatable* and *inflation* are **synonyms**.

2. T F *Inflate* and *deflate* are **antonyms**.

3. T F *Interstellar* means "**between the seasons.**"

4. T F In the words *tricycle* and *triangle*, "*tri-*" means "**three.**"

5. T F **Prefixes** always change **nouns** to **verbs**.

#024. Prefixes 8

List a word for each prefix. Then give a brief definition for each new word. Use a dictionary to check your answers.

1. *circum-* (around) _____
   _____

2. *contra-* (against) _____
   _____

3. *de-* (down or from) _____
   _____

4. *tele-* (far) _____
   _____

5. *retro-* (backward) _____
   _____

CD-404245 ©Mark Twain Media, Inc., Publishers

Root Words, Prefixes, and Suffixes

#025. Prefixes With Negative Meanings 1

Consider the meaning of these words:

unlike	illogic
inappropriate	inconsiderate
disappear	disadvantage
nonprofit	nonsense
improbable	impossible

What do the prefixes **un-**, **il-**, **in-**, **im-**, **non-**, and **dis-** have in common?

_____

_____

#026. Prefixes With Negative Meanings 2

Add the prefix **un-** to the root words given. Write the new word. Then write a short definition for each word that doesn't include the word **not**. Example: **un** + **happy** = **unhappy**: sad

1. able _____

_____

2. like _____

_____

3. do _____

_____

4. made _____

_____

5. cover _____

_____

#027. Prefixes With Negative Meanings 3

Write words from the list to match the definitions. Keep in mind the meaning of the prefix and the root words.

disable	disarm	discharge
discolored	disloyal	disorder
disrespect	disrepair	

_____ 1. falling apart
_____ 2. make harmless
_____ 3. chaos
_____ 4. false
_____ 5. make useless
_____ 6. stained
_____ 7. release from duty
_____ 8. rudeness

#028. Prefixes With Negative Meanings 4

1. How can knowing the meaning of a **prefix** and the **root word** help you understand the meaning of a new word?

_____

_____

_____

2. If you know the meaning of the **prefix**, but not the **root word**, how can that help you understand the meaning of the new word?

_____

_____

_____

Root Words, Prefixes, and Suffixes

#029. Prefixes With Negative Meanings 5

Add the prefix **un-** or **dis-** to each word. Write the new words, then use the new words in a sentence.

1. **trust** _____
_____
_____

2. **true** _____
_____
_____

3. **obey** _____
_____
_____

4. **bearable** _____
_____
_____

#030. Prefixes With Negative Meanings 6

The prefixes **dis-, in-, il-, im-, non-,** and **un-** change a word so that it means the opposite. Write definitions for the underlined words without using the word **not**.

1. **Finite** means limited. What does **infinite** mean? _____
_____

2. **Appropriate** means right or correct. What does **inappropriate** mean?
_____

3. **Patient** means calm and accepting. What does **impatient** mean?
_____

4. **Logical** means reasonable. What does **illogical** mean?
_____

#031. Prefixes With Negative Meanings 7

Circle 16 words that begin with **un-** in the puzzle. List the words on your own paper.

```
L N U L U U D E S U N U
A W U U A R N U U N N E
U O D U I E N R O B N U
S N E A V U R T E O U L
U K F E U N U N C L O G
N N N I N U D U U T U N
U U U N T I E D A M N U
```

UN = NOT

#032. Prefixes With Negative Meanings 8

Write the letter of the answer that best matches the meaning of the word.

_____ 1. not needed
   A. **necessary**   B. **unnecessary**

_____ 2. not truthful
   A. **dishonest**   B. **disbelief**

_____ 3. unwanted
   A. **undesirable**   B. **desirable**

_____ 4. to stop
   A. **unavailable**   B. **discontinue**

_____ 5. without end
   A. **limited**   B. **unlimited**

Root Words, Prefixes, and Suffixes

#033. Prefixes With Negative Meanings 9

Add *dis-* to each word. Write a sentence using each new word.

1. advantage _____
   _____
   _____
2. approve _____
   _____
   _____
3. connect _____
   _____
   _____
4. prove _____
   _____
   _____

#034. Prefixes With Negative Meanings 10

Answer the questions.

1. **Comply** means obey. What does **non-compliance** mean? _____
   _____
2. Give an example of a **nonprofit** organization.
   _____
3. **Toxic** means poisonous. What does **non-toxic** mean? _____
   _____
4. Give an example of a **nondairy** product.
   _____
5. Give an example of a **nonfiction** book.
   _____

#035. Prefixes With Negative Meanings 11

Write the letter of the answer that best matches the meaning of the word.

____ 1. **disadvantage**   A. dislike
____ 2. **discontinue**   B. not having
____ 3. **disconnect**   the same
____ 4. **disagree**   opinion
____ 5. **disapprove**   C. release
____ 6. **discharge**   D. stop
                              E. difficulty
                              F. take apart

#036. Prefixes With Negative Meanings 12

Answer the following questions.

1. What does it mean to **mistype** a word on the computer? _____
   _____
2. If someone wears **mismatched** socks, what's the problem? _____
   _____
3. If someone **misleads** you when you ask for directions, what could happen?
   _____
   _____
4. What can happen if a student **misbehaves** in school? _____
   _____

Language Arts Warm-Ups: Expanding Vocabulary   Root Words, Prefixes, and Suffixes

Name: _____ Date: _____

Root Words, Prefixes, and Suffixes

#037. Prefixes Denoting Numbers 1

On your own paper, write a poem using the prefixes for the numbers one through ten as the first part of each line. Use "One, Two, Buckle My Shoe" as a model. Be as silly as you like.

Example: **Unicorns**, **bipeds**, give it a try.

Number Prefixes
uni-, bi-
tri-, quadri-
penta-, hexa-
sept-, octa-
nona-, deca-

#038. Prefixes Denoting Numbers 2

Match the words from the list to the definitions.

centennial   hexagon
octopus   triceratops

1. a shape with 6 sides
   _____

2. a dinosaur with 3 horns
   _____

3. an animal with 8 arms
   _____

4. a 100-year celebration
   _____

#039. Prefixes Denoting Numbers 3

Write the words from the list to match the definitions.

bimonthly   decathlon
quadruplets quintet

1. 10-sport Olympic event
   _____

2. 4 of the same
   _____

3. 5 musicians
   _____

4. every 2 months
   _____

#040. Prefixes Denoting Numbers 4

1. How many sides does a **decagon** have?
   _____

2. Which is longer, a meter or a **millimeter**?
   _____

3. How many **millimeters** are in a meter?
   _____

4. Which is longer, a meter or a **centimeter**?
   _____

5. How many **centimeters** are in a meter?
   _____

6. How many **milliliters** are in a liter?
   _____

Language Arts Warm-Ups: Expanding Vocabulary   Root Words, Prefixes, and Suffixes

Name: _____ Date: _____

Root Words, Prefixes, and Suffixes

#041. Prefixes Denoting Numbers 5

Circle the correct words to match the definitions. Knowing what the prefixes mean will help.

1. Knowing two languages
   bilateral   **bilingual**   **bicycle**
2. Five Olympic sporting events
   quintuplet   **pentagon**   **pentathlon**
3. A 200-year celebration
   centennial   **biannual**   **bicentennial**
4. A set of three related books or movies
   tripod   **trilogy**   **triangle**
5. To cut into two pieces
   divide   **bisect**   **bicycle**
6. Three of the same
   triangle   **triplets**   **triceratops**
7. The eighth month in the Roman calendar
   October   **August**   **December**

#042. Prefixes Denoting Numbers 6

1. If you received the first issue of a **bimonthly** magazine in May, when should the next one arrive? _____
2. If a school held a **biannual** event in May of 2016, when would the next one be held? _____
3. If a family met for a **biennial** reunion in July, 2016, when did the last reunion occur? _____
4. How often do you think a **century** plant blooms? _____
5. When will the **tricentennial** celebration of the United States as a country be held? _____

#043. Prefixes Denoting Numbers 7

1. Which has more legs, a **centipede** or a **millipede**? _____
2. How many years are in a **millennium**? _____
3. How many soldiers do you think a Roman **centurion** commanded? _____
4. Why are some types of eyeglasses called **bifocals**? _____

#044. Prefixes Denoting Numbers 8

Write the **prefix** for each number, and list a word with that prefix.

1 _____
2 _____
3 _____
4 _____
5 _____
6 _____
8 _____
10 _____
100 _____
1,000 _____

Language Arts Warm-Ups: Expanding Vocabulary   Root Words, Prefixes, and Suffixes

Name: _____ Date: _____

Root Words, Prefixes, and Suffixes

#045. Prefixes over- and under- 1

As a prefix, **under-** can mean:
   A. beneath; below
   B. lower in rank
   C. not enough.

For each word, write "A," "B," or "C" to indicate how the prefix **under-** is used.

1. _____ underground
2. _____ underclassman
3. _____ undersecretary
4. _____ underdeveloped
5. _____ underpaid
6. _____ underline

#046. Prefixes over- and under- 2

As a prefix, **over-** can have two different meanings.

1. Write five words that begin with the prefix **over-** meaning **greatly** or **completely**. *Example:* **overjoyed**
   _____
   _____
   _____

2. Write five words that begin with the prefix **over-** meaning **upper**, **outer**, or **above**. *Example:* **overcoat**
   _____
   _____
   _____

#047. Prefixes in-, im-, and ex- 1

1. **Inhale** means to breathe in. What does **exhale** mean?
   _____

2. **Include** means to take in. What does **exclude** mean?
   _____

3. **Implode** means to burst inward. What does **explode** mean?
   _____

4. Give a one-word definition of the prefix **ex-**.
   _____

#048. Prefixes in-, im-, and ex- 2

Answer below. Use a dictionary if you aren't sure of the answers.

1. What is the difference between **incite** and **excite**?
   _____
   _____

2. What is the difference between **import** and **export**?
   _____
   _____

3. What is the difference between **expire** and **inspire**?
   _____
   _____

Root Words, Prefixes, and Suffixes

#049. Prefixes Denoting Size and Position 1

The prefix *hemi-* comes from the Greek word meaning **half**. The prefix *semi-* comes from the Latin word meaning **half** or **partly**. Write the answers below.

1. Draw a **semicircle**.

2. Do you live in the northern or southern **hemisphere**? _____

3. What does it mean to have a **semiprivate** room in a hospital? _____

#050. Prefixes Denoting Size and Position 2

Micro- and *macro-* are prefixes that mean the opposite. The prefix *macro-* means **huge**, as in, *The universe is a **macrocosm**.*

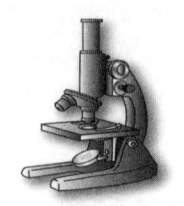

1. What does the prefix *micro-* mean? _____

2. What is a **microcosm**? _____

3. What does a **microscope** do? _____

#051. Prefixes Denoting Size and Position 3

The prefix *extra-* means **outside** or **beyond**. Write your answers below. Use a dictionary if you need help.

1. When astronauts go outside of a spacecraft in space, it's called an **EVA**. What does **EVA** stand for? _____

2. Some people believe they have **ESP**. What does **ESP** stand for? _____

3. In the movie *E.T.*, what does **ET** stand for? _____

#052. Prefixes Denoting Size and Position 4

The prefixes *hyper-* and *hypo-* mean the opposite. A person who is **hyperactive** is extremely active—far above the usual. A person who is **hypoactive** may move very little.

1. Which prefix means more than normal? _____

2. Which prefix means less than usual? _____

3. Would a **hypersonic** sound be very loud or very soft? _____

4. When a person suffers from **hypothermia**, would his temperature be high or low? _____

Language Arts Warm-Ups: Expanding Vocabulary　　　Root Words, Prefixes, and Suffixes

Name: _____　Date: _____

Root Words, Prefixes, and Suffixes

#053. Prefixes Denoting Size and Position 5

As a prefix, *sub-* can mean: A. under, less, or at a lower position; B. lower in rank; or C. nearly or approximately. For each word, write "A," "B," or "C" to indicate how the prefix *sub-* is used. Use a dictionary if you need help.

1. **submarine** _____
2. **subtropical** _____
3. **subsoil** _____
4. **subway** _____
5. **subcommittee** _____
6. **subdivide** _____
7. **subheading** _____
8. **subtotal** _____

#054. Prefixes Denoting Size and Position 6

The prefix *inter-* means **between** or **among**. The prefix *intra-* means **inside** or **within**. Circle the correct word for each item.

1. To exchange gifts between two people: **interchange** or **intrachange**
2. Sporting events between teams from different schools: **intermural** or **intramural**
3. Sporting events between teams in the same school: **intermural** or **intramural**
4. A highway that covers more than one state: **interstate** or **intrastate**
5. Shipping from one city to another inside the same state: **interstate** or **intrastate**
6. A flight from New York to London: **intercontinental** or **intracontinental**

#055. Prefixes Denoting Size and Position 17

The prefix *mega-* can mean either **1,000 of something** or **very large**.

1. There are about 1,000 species of bats. They are divided into two groups: **megabats** and **microbats**. Which group represents the larger bats?
   _____
2. How many bytes are in a **megabyte**?
   _____
3. Write another word that begins with the prefix *mega-*.
   _____

#056. Prefixes Denoting Size and Position 8

The prefix *de-* can mean **down** or **away**. It can also mean to **remove** or **reverse**. Write a short definition for each word. Use a dictionary if you need help.

1. **descend** _____
2. **debug** _____
3. **delay** _____
4. **deduce** _____
5. **decline** _____
6. **demerit** _____
7. **deduct** _____

Language Arts Warm-Ups: Expanding Vocabulary   Root Words, Prefixes, and Suffixes

Name: _____   Date: _____

Root Words, Prefixes, and Suffixes

#057. Prefix Review 1

Divide a sheet of paper into four columns. Write words that begin with a different **prefix** in each column. Select any prefixes to use. Try to list at least ten words for each prefix.

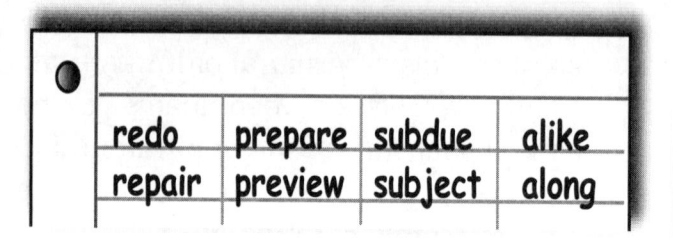

| redo | prepare | subdue | alike |
| repair | preview | subject | along |

#058. Prefix Review 2

Match the definitions to the prefixes from this list.

| pre- | over- | macro- | sub- |
| micro- | hyper- | re- | mis- |

1. before _____
2. huge _____
3. not _____
4. tiny _____
5. again _____
6. above _____
7. more than normal _____
8. lower in rank or below _____

#059. Prefix Review 3

Write one of these prefixes on the blank before each word to make a new word. Some root words may work with more than one prefix.

1. _____activate
2. _____state
3. _____formed
4. _____ordinary
5. _____part
6. _____phone
7. _____port
8. _____active

de-
ex-
extra-
hyper-
hypo-
inter-
intra-
macro-
mega-
micro-

#060. Prefix Review 4

Circle the prefix in each word. Underline the root words.

1. **disagree**   2. **distrust**
3. **insincere**   4. **incorrect**
5. **indirect**   6. **immortal**
7. **impolite**   8. **misfit**
9. **mistrust**   10. **nonstop**
11. **nonprofit**   12. **overhead**
13. **overheat**   14. **overweight**
15. **unhappy**   16. **unselfish**
17. **underfoot**   18. **underline**
19. **replace**   20. **illegal**

CD-404245 ©Mark Twain Media, Inc., Publishers   16

Language Arts Warm-Ups: Expanding Vocabulary   Root Words, Prefixes, and Suffixes

Name: _____ Date: _____

Root Words, Prefixes, and Suffixes

#061. Prefix Review 5

Write ten words using a prefix that has a number meaning, such as *tri-* or *quad-*. On your own paper, write a short definition for each word.

1. _____
2. _____
3. _____
4. _____
5. _____
6. _____
7. _____
8. _____
9. _____
10. _____

#062. Prefix Review 6

Add **un-**, **dis-**, **in-**, **il-**, or **im-** to each adjective. Write a short sentence for each new word that shows you understand the meaning of the word. Use a dictionary if needed.

1. _____**familiar** _____
_____
2. _____**formal** _____
_____
3. _____**legible** _____
_____
4. _____**practical** _____
_____
5. _____**satisfied** _____
_____
6. _____**tolerable** _____
_____

#063. Prefix Review 7

Does the word contain a prefix? Write "yes" or "no" on the line.

_____ 1. **uncle**
_____ 2. **illness**
_____ 3. **uncap**
_____ 4. **illogical**
_____ 5. **unclear**
_____ 6. **dishes**
_____ 7. **unite**
_____ 8. **distrust**
_____ 9. **untie**
_____ 10. **misses**
_____ 11. **ready**
_____ 12. **none**

#064. Prefix Review 8

Explain the difference between each pair of words.

1. **miscalculate** and **recalculate**
_____
_____
2. **disorder** and **reorder** _____
_____
3. **bicentennial** and **biannual** _____
_____
4. **removed** and **unmoved** _____
_____
5. **pentathlon** and **decathlon** _____
_____

CD-404245 ©Mark Twain Media, Inc., Publishers   17

Language Arts Warm-Ups: Expanding Vocabulary

Root Words, Prefixes, and Suffixes

Name: _____ Date: _____

Root Words, Prefixes, and Suffixes

#065. Prefix Review 9

Add a prefix to each root word. On your own paper, use each new word in a sentence.

1. _____loyal
2. _____annual
3. _____color
4. _____cycle
5. _____sphere
6. _____done
7. _____use
8. _____think
9. _____paint
10. _____place

#066. Prefix Review 10

Match the words and definitions.

___ 1. **dissatisfied**   A. harm
___ 2. **impossible**   B. below the water
___ 3. **impractical**   C. new and strange
___ 4. **insincere**   D. unhappy
___ 5. **misshapen**   E. twisted
___ 6. **mistreat**   F. can't happen
___ 7. **undersea**   G. not truthful
___ 8. **unfamiliar**   H. not useful

#067. Prefix Review 11

1. Which are larger: **microorganisms** or **macroorganisms**? _____
2. If you **export** goods, does it mean you buy from or sell to another country? _____
3. Would a flight from Canada to Mexico be **intercontinental** or **intracontinental**? _____
4. Would **megasaurus** be a good name for a small dinosaur? _____
5. An example of an **interplanetary** trip would be from _____ to _____.

#068. Prefix Review 12

Circle "T" for true or "F" for false.

1. T F The meaning of a word changes when a **prefix** is added.
2. T F **Prefixes** only appear at the beginning of words.
3. T F Adding a **prefix** usually changes the part of speech of a word.
4. T F A word cannot include both a **prefix** and a **suffix**.
5. T F A **prefix** is added to the end of a word.
6. T F A word can have two or more **prefixes**.
7. T F The spelling of a **root word** usually doesn't change when a **prefix** is added.

Language Arts Warm-Ups: Expanding Vocabulary   Root Words, Prefixes, and Suffixes

Name: _____   Date: _____

Root Words, Prefixes, and Suffixes

#069. Suffixes 1

A **suffix** is added to the end of a word and changes its meaning. Adding a suffix sometimes changes the spelling of the root word. The suffix *-less* means **without**. The suffix *-some* means **full** or **like**. Add the suffix *-less* or *-some* to each word. Write a brief definition for each new word. Use a dictionary to check answers.

1. **home** _____ _____
   _____

2. **awe** _____ _____
   _____

3. **sense** _____ _____
   _____

4. **fear** _____ _____
   _____

#070. Suffixes 2

The suffix *-ment* means the **act of** or **state of something**; *-ible* and *-able* both mean **able to**. Add one of these suffixes to the underlined root word in each sentence to fill in the blank.

1. Everyone **loved** the new puppy; it was so _____.

2. Dan didn't want to **retire** because he couldn't afford _____ yet.

3. Everyone knew Paul was _____ because he had a lot of common **sense**.

#071. Suffixes 3

Circle "T" for true or "F" for false. Use a dictionary to check your answers.

1. T   F   **Suffixes** can completely change the meaning of words.

2. T   F   **Suffixes** are added to the beginning of a word.

3. T   F   The spelling of a **root word** never changes when **suffixes** are added.

#072. Suffixes 4

Write sentences using any word that ends with each suffix listed.

1. *-able* _____
   _____

2. *-ible* _____
   _____

3. *-some* _____
   _____

4. *-ish* _____
   _____

5. *-ment* _____
   _____

6. *-al* _____

Language Arts Warm-Ups: Expanding Vocabulary

Root Words, Prefixes, and Suffixes

Name: _____ Date: _____

Root Words, Prefixes, and Suffixes

#073. Suffixes 5

List a word for each suffix. Give a brief definition for each new word.

1. *-ship* _____
   _____
   _____

2. *-ance* _____
   _____
   _____

3. *-ish* _____
   _____
   _____

#074. Suffixes 6

Answer the following questions.

1. How can knowing the meaning of a **suffix** help us figure out the meaning of a new word?
   _____
   _____
   _____

2. Use a dictionary to explain the difference in meaning between **democracy** and **demographic**.
   _____
   _____
   _____
   _____

#075. Suffixes 7

Write the root words for each word in the parentheses. Then match the words with their definitions. Feel free to use a dictionary.

____ 1. **presentation** (_____)
____ 2. **selection** (_____)
____ 3. **exploration** (_____)
____ 4. **appreciation** (_____)
____ 5. **reflection** (_____)
____ 6. **election** (_____)

A. mirror image   B. discovery
C. choosing a candidate D. choice
E. gratitude   F. demonstration

#076. Suffixes 8

Circle "T" for true or "F" for false. Use a dictionary to check your answers.

1. T F **Inflatable** and **inflation** are synonyms.
2. T F **Childish** and **childlike** are antonyms.
3. T F **Imitation**, **celebration**, and **conversation** are verbs.
4. T F In the words **biology**, **astrology**, and **geology**, *-ology* means *the study of*.
5. T F Suffixes always change verbs to nouns.

Language Arts Warm-Ups: Expanding Vocabulary   Root Words, Prefixes, and Suffixes

Name: _____   Date: _____

Root Words, Prefixes, and Suffixes

#077. Adding Suffixes 1

Adding a suffix to a root word changes the meaning of the word. Sometimes the spelling of the root word also changes. Write two examples for each rule below.

- For words ending in **e**, drop the **e** and add the suffix if the suffix begins with a vowel. *Example:* expire + ation = expiration

1. _____
   _____

- For short words with the **consonant/vowel/consonant** (**CVC**) pattern, double the final consonant before adding the suffix. *Example:* hot + est = hottest

2. _____
   _____

#078. Adding Suffixes 2

Write two more examples of each rule.

- For most words ending in **y** preceded by a vowel, simply add the suffix. *Example:* buy + er = buyer

1. _____
   _____

- For most words ending in **y** preceded by a consonant, change the **y** to **i** and add the suffix. *Example:* try + ed = tried

2. _____
   _____

#079. Adding Suffixes 3

Circle the root words if the spelling will change when a suffix beginning with a vowel is added. Then pick two of the words and use them in a sentence below.

beauty	big	bumpy	busy
carry	desire	direct	tall
fluffy	wet	greasy	magnify
rapid	short	slow	ugly

1. _____
   _____
2. _____
   _____

#080. Adding Suffixes 4

Write the root word for each word below. Use a dictionary if needed.

1. adoption   _____
2. agreement   _____
3. stylish   _____
4. combination   _____
5. daily   _____
6. decoration   _____
7. directions   _____
8. government   _____
9. invitation   _____
10. twitching   _____

Language Arts Warm-Ups: Expanding Vocabulary   Root Words, Prefixes, and Suffixes

Name: _____   Date: _____

Root Words, Prefixes, and Suffixes

#081. Suffixes -er, -or, -est 1

When the suffix *-er* is added to an adjective, it means **more**. Review spelling rules. Add *-er* to each word, and write new words. *Example:* quick + er = quicker

1. hot _____
2. sad _____
3. cold _____
4. tasty _____
5. funny _____
6. red _____
7. high _____
8. dry _____

#082. Suffixes -er, -or, -est 2

When the suffix *-est* is added to an adjective, it means **most**. Review spelling rules. Add *-est* and write the new words. *Example:* quick + est = quickest

1. speedy _____
2. wise _____
3. close _____
4. jolly _____
5. tiny _____
6. wet _____
7. fresh _____
8. old _____
9. spicy _____
10. When *-est* is added to an **adjective**, is the new word an **adjective**? _____

#083. Suffixes -er, -or, -est 3

Adding the suffix *-er* or *-or* to a **verb** changes it to a **noun**. Add *-er* or *-or* to each verb, and write the new words. Review spelling rules. Check a dictionary if you are not sure which suffix to use. *Examples:* act + or = actor, play + er = player

1. bake _____
2. direct _____
3. golf _____
4. govern _____
5. jog _____
6. sing _____
7. manage _____
8. write _____

#084. Suffixes -er, -or, -est 4

1. What do the suffixes *-er* and *-or* mean?
_____
_____

2. Write ten other **verbs** not used in Activity #144 that change to **nouns** by adding *-er* or *-or*.
_____
_____
_____
_____
_____

CD-404245 ©Mark Twain Media, Inc., Publishers   22

Language Arts Warm-Ups: Expanding Vocabulary   Root Words, Prefixes, and Suffixes

Name: _____   Date: _____

Root Words, Prefixes, and Suffixes

#085. Suffixes -ly and -ful 1

Adding the suffix **-ly** to an **adjective** changes it to an **adverb**. Write the adverb form of each word. Then write a short sentence for each of the words on your own paper.

1. **broad** _____
2. **polite** _____
3. **quick** _____
4. **quiet** _____
5. **rude** _____
6. **sad** _____
7. **shy** _____
8. **silent** _____
9. **timid** _____
10. **weak** _____

#086. Suffixes -ly and -ful 2

The words **thoughtful**, **trustful**, and **handful** include the suffix **-ful**.

1. What does the suffix **-ful** mean? _____
   _____

2. Write six more words that end with the suffix **-ful**. _____
   _____
   _____

3. Write a sentence using two words that end in **-ful**. _____
   _____
   _____

#087. Suffixes -ly and -ful 3

Add the suffix **-ful** to each of these words, and then use the new words in a sentence.

1. **color** _____
   _____
   _____

2. **grace** _____
   _____
   _____

3. **plenty** _____
   _____
   _____

4. **play** _____
   _____
   _____

#088. Suffixes -ly and -ful 4

Match the words ending in **-ful** with their definitions. Use a dictionary if needed.

____ 1. **boastful**   A. honest
____ 2. **cheerful**   B. imaginative
____ 3. **doubtful**   C. sad
____ 4. **dreadful**   D. risky
____ 5. **dutiful**   E. tasty
____ 6. **fanciful**   F. proud
____ 7. **flavorful**   G. terrible
____ 8. **tearful**   H. happy
____ 9. **truthful**   I. unsure
____ 10. **harmful**   J. obedient

Language Arts Warm-Ups: Expanding VocabularyRoot Words, Prefixes, and Suffixes

Name: _____ Date: _____

Root Words, Prefixes, and Suffixes

#089. Suffixes -less, -tion, -ation 1

The words **helpless**, **fearless**, and **friendless** include the suffix *-less*.

1. What does the suffix *-less* mean? _____
   _____
   _____

Write four more words that end in *-less*. Include a short definition for each word.

2. _____ _____
   _____
3. _____ _____
   _____
4. _____ _____
   _____
5. _____ _____
   _____

#090. Suffixes -less, -tion, -ation 2

1. Do you prefer foods that are **tasteless** or **tasteful**? _____

2. Is a good dancer **graceless** or **graceful**?
   _____

3. Are you a **careless** person or a **careful** one? _____

4. Does **endless** mean eternal or brief?
   _____

5. If something is **flawless**, does it have few errors or no errors? _____

6. Why were early cars called "**horseless** carriages"? _____
   _____
   _____

#091. Suffixes -less, -tion, -ation 3

The suffixes *-tion* and *-ation* change words from **verbs** to **nouns**. *Example: adore + ation = adoration.* Add *-tion* or *-ation* to each verb, and then write a short definition for the word. Use a dictionary if you are unsure of the spelling or definition.

1. **donate** _____
   _____
2. **admire** _____
   _____
3. **regulate** _____
   _____
4. **cooperate** _____
   _____
5. **inspire** _____
   _____

#092. Suffixes -less, -tion, -ation 4

Match the words to their definitions. Use a dictionary if you need help.

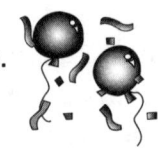

___ 1. **adopt**
___ 2. **invite**
___ 3. **adoption**
___ 4. **educate**
___ 5. **decorate**
___ 6. **decorations**
___ 7. **education**
___ 8. **invitation**

A. the process of learning
B. to ask
C. ornaments
D. to make something look nice
E. to teach
F. a request to attend or meet
G. to acquire
H. the bringing of a child into one's family

CD-404245 ©Mark Twain Media, Inc., Publishers24

Root Words, Prefixes, and Suffixes

#093. Suffixes -able and -ment 1

Acceptable, *workable*, and *taxable* end with the suffix *-able*. Add the suffix *-able* to each word below, and write the new word. Keep spelling guidelines in mind.

1. **avoid** _____
2. **bear** _____
3. **bend** _____
4. **compare** _____
5. **inflate** _____
6. **like** _____
7. **love** _____
8. **remove** _____
9. **respect** _____
10. **use** _____
11. What does the suffix *-able* mean?
    _____

#094. Suffixes -able and -ment 2

1. Name something that is **chewable**.
   _____
2. Give an example of something people wear that is **fashionable**.
   _____
3. Name an organization that is **charitable**.
   _____
4. What kind of weather is **favorable** for a parade?
   _____
5. What does "**payable** on demand" mean?
   _____
6. What would you like to have that is not **affordable** to you right now?
   _____

#095. Suffixes -able and -ment 3

Adding the suffix *-ment* changes words from **verbs** to **nouns**. Add *-ment* to each word. Write the new word. On your own paper, write a short definition for each word.

1. **adjust** _____
2. **advertise** _____
3. **amuse** _____
4. **assign** _____
5. **excite** _____
6. **judge** _____
7. **manage** _____
8. **pay** _____

#096. Suffixes -able and -ment 4

1. Give an example of something that would cause **excitement** in your school.
   _____
2. Name one type of **treatment** for a cold.
   _____
3. Name something about which you and your parents are in **agreement**.
   _____
4. Name something that causes you **amazement**.
   _____
5. What is something you feel is a great **accomplishment**?
   _____

Language Arts Warm-Ups: Expanding Vocabulary   Root Words, Prefixes, and Suffixes

Name: _____   Date: _____

Root Words, Prefixes, and Suffixes

#097. Suffixes -ology, -ist, -phobia 1

The suffix **-ology** means the **study of**. Use a dictionary or the Internet to find out about these **-ologies**.

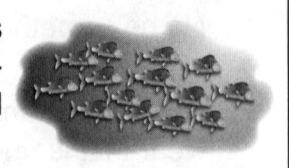

Example: **Criminology** is the study of crimes and criminals.

1. **Biology** is the study of _____.
2. **Zoology** is the study of _____.
3. **Mythology** is the study of _____.
4. **Geology** is the study of _____.
5. **Anthropology** is the study of _____.
6. **Psychology** is the study of _____.
7. **Archaeology** is the study of _____.
8. **Ichthyology** is the study of _____.

#098. Suffixes -ology, -ist, -phobia 2

The suffix **-ist** often means **someone who knows how to do something**.

Example: A **flutist** knows how to play a flute.

1. A **botanist** is one who knows about _____.
2. A **florist** knows about _____.
3. A **dentist** takes care of _____.
4. A **harpist** knows how to play the _____.
5. A person who has studied **biology** would be a _____.

#099. Suffixes -ology, -ist, -phobia 3

1. What subject does a **chemist** know about? _____
2. What does a **cyclist** ride? _____
3. What is the word for someone who plays the piano? _____
4. What does a **therapist** do? _____
5. What does a **typist** do well? _____
6. What does a **meteorologist** study? _____

#100. Suffixes -ology, -ist, -phobia 4

The suffix **-phobia** means **fear of** something. Use a dictionary or the Internet to find out about these **phobias**.

1. **Acrophobia** means fear of _____.
2. **Apiphobia** means fear of _____.
3. **Hydrophobia** means fear of _____.
4. **Heliophobia** means fear of _____.
5. **Phobophobia** means fear of _____.

Language Arts Warm-Ups: Expanding Vocabulary Root Words, Prefixes, and Suffixes

Name: _____ Date: _____

Root Words, Prefixes, and Suffixes

#101. Suffixes -ish, -ness, -an 1

Add the suffix *-ish* to each word. Write a short definition for the new words.

1. baby _____
2. blue _____
3. child _____
4. green _____
5. red _____
6. style _____

#102. Suffixes -ish, -ness, -an 2

Add the suffix *-ness* to each word and write the new word. Review spelling guidelines for words ending in *y*. Write a short definition for the new words.

1. dizzy _____
2. easy _____
3. firm _____
4. lazy _____
5. lonely _____
6. meek _____

#103. Suffixes -ish, -ness, -an 3

The suffixes *-ish* and *-an*, combined with part of a country name, are commonly used to denote **nationality** or **language**. *Example:* A person from Great Britain is **British**. Use a dictionary if you need help.

1. A person from Sweden is _____.
2. A person from Australia is _____.
3. In Turkey, people speak _____.
4. People from Finland speak _____.
5. People from Rome were called _____.

#104. Suffixes -ish, -ness, -an 4

1. The language of Spain is _____.
2. People from Egypt are _____.
3. In Italy, people speak _____.
4. People from Hawaii are _____.
5. People in Russia speak _____.
6. People from Poland speak _____.
7. A person from Mexico is _____.
8. People from Ireland are _____.

Language Arts Warm-Ups: Expanding Vocabulary   Root Words, Prefixes, and Suffixes

Name: _____ Date: _____

Root Words, Prefixes, and Suffixes

#105. Suffix Review 1

Does the spelling of the root word change when the suffix is added? Circle "yes" or "no." If yes, write the new word.

1. **beauty** + *-ful*   yes   no
   _____

2. **desire** + *-able*   yes   no
   _____

3. **equip** + *-ment*   yes   no
   _____

4. **except** + *-ion*   yes   no
   _____

5. **happy** + *-ly*   yes   no
   _____

6. **icy** + *-est*   yes   no
   _____

#106. Suffix Review 2

Circle the 21 *-er* and *-or* words hidden in the puzzle.

V	D	I	N	E	R	E	K	A	B
E	O	A	R	A	R	E	C	A	R
N	E	T	N	E	R	T	R	A	B
D	R	G	E	C	O	B	M	E	W
O	E	O	R	R	E	V	A	E	W
R	L	R	O	R	R	R	Y	D	E
E	D	R	O	V	E	R	O	I	L
V	D	N	F	R	X	E	R	T	D
I	O	R	E	M	R	A	F	O	E
D	T	A	R	E	T	N	E	R	R

ACTOR   BAKER   BARBER   BEARER
DANCER   DINER   DIVER   DONOR
EDITOR   FARMER   MAYOR   RACER
RANGER   RENTER   ROVER   ROOFER
TODDLER   VENDOR   VOTER   WEAVER
WELDER

#107. Suffix Review 3

On your own paper, write three couplets (two-line rhyming poems) using words that end in *-er* or *-or*.

Examples:

The **miner** felt **finer**
After he ate at the **diner**.

I said to the **baker**,
"Please pass the salt **shaker**."

#108. Suffix Review 4

Circle "T" for true or "F" for false.

1. T F A **proposition** is a **suggestion** or **plan**.

2. T F **To observe** can mean **to watch the stars**.

3. T F **To be observant** means **to pay attention to details**.

4. T F A **proposal** is a **promise**.

5. T F An **observer** is **one who is lost**.

6. T F **To propose** means **to ask someone to marry you**.

CD-404245 ©Mark Twain Media, Inc., Publishers   28

Root Words, Prefixes, and Suffixes

#109. Suffix Review 5

Write the answers from the list of suffixes.

-able	-er	-ful	-ish
-less	-ly	-ology	-phobia

_____ 1. Suffix that changes **adjectives** to **adverbs**

_____ 2. Suffix that means **able to**

_____ 3. Suffix that means **somewhat like**

_____ 4. Suffix that means **fear of**

_____ 5. Suffix that means **filled with**

_____ 6. Suffix that means **lack of**

_____ 7. Suffix that means **one who**

_____ 8. Suffix that means **study of**

#110. Suffix Review 6

1. When **-er** or **-or** is added to a verb, is the new word a **verb** or a **noun**?

2. Write two examples of question 1.

3. When **-er** is added to an adjective, is the new word an **adjective** or an **adverb**?

4. Write two examples of question 3.

5. When **-est** is added to an adjective, is the new word a **noun** or an **adjective**?

6. Write two examples of question 5.

#111. Suffix Review 7

1. When **-ly** is added to an adjective, is the new word an **adverb** or an **adjective**?

2. Write two examples of question 1.

3. When **-tion** or **-ation** is added to a verb, is the new word an **adjective** or a **noun**?

4. Write two examples of question 3.

5. When **-ment** is added to a verb, is the new word a **verb** or a **noun**?

6. Write two examples of question 5.

#112. Suffix Review 8

On the tree branches, write five or more words made by adding **prefixes** and/or **suffixes** to the root word.

PAY

Language Arts Warm-Ups: Expanding Vocabulary   Root Words, Prefixes, and Suffixes

Name: _____ Date: _____

Root Words, Prefixes, and Suffixes

#113. Words With Prefixes & Suffixes 1

Underline the prefixes and suffixes in each word. Write the root words on the lines.

1. **direction** _____
2. **directory** _____
3. **investigate** _____
4. **investigator** _____
5. **observance** _____
6. **observatory** _____
7. **observer** _____
8. **proposal** _____
9. **proposition** _____
10. **reinvest** _____

#114. Words With Prefixes & Suffixes 2

Add a prefix and one or more suffixes to each word. Write the new words, then write a short definition for the word. Use a dictionary if you are unsure of the spelling or definition.
Example: un + luck + y = unlucky

1. **like** _____
   _____
2. **happy** _____
   _____
3. **invest** _____
   _____
4. **detect** _____
   _____
5. **cooperate** _____
   _____

#115. Words With Prefixes & Suffixes 3

On the tree branches, write five or more words made by adding **prefixes** and/or **suffixes** to the root word.

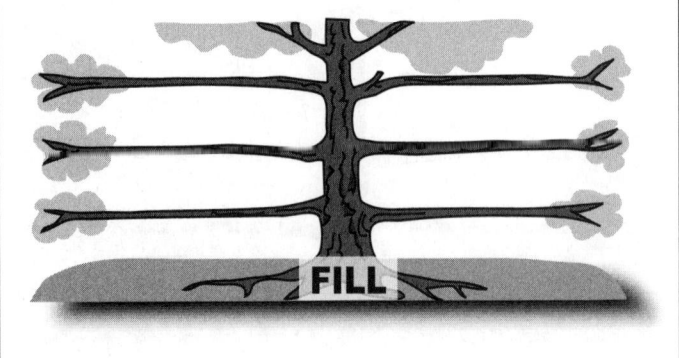

(tree with FILL as the root)

#116. Words With Prefixes & Suffixes 4

Write the letter of the correct word for each definition given.

____ 1. a great amount
  A. **reconsider**   B. **considerable**
____ 2. a joint effort
  A. **cooperate**   B. **cooperation**
____ 3. on the other hand
  A. **alteration**   B. **alternately**
____ 4. selfish
  A. **inconsiderate**   B. **reconsider**
____ 5. unchanged
  A. **altered**   B. **unaltered**
____ 6. unhelpful
  A. **cooperative** B. **uncooperative**
____ 7. unnoticeable
  A. **undetectable**   B. **detection**

CD-404245 ©Mark Twain Media, Inc., Publishers

Language Arts Warm-Ups: Expanding VocabularyRoot Words, Prefixes, and Suffixes

Name: _____ Date: _____

Root Words, Prefixes, and Suffixes

#117. Words With Prefixes & Suffixes 5

On the tree branches, write five or more words made by adding **prefixes** and/or **suffixes** to the root word.

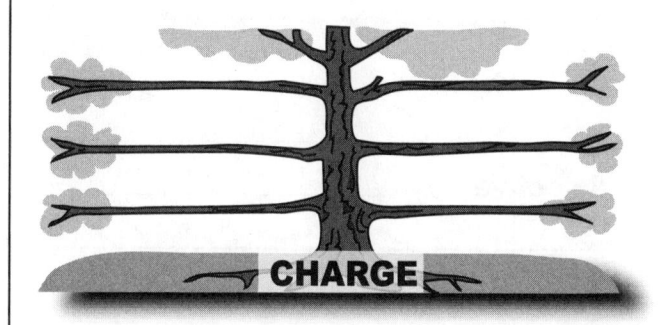

(Tree labeled CHARGE)

#118. Words With Prefixes & Suffixes 6

Adding prefixes and suffixes changes the part of speech of a word. Write "N" if the word is a **noun**, "V" if it is a **verb**, or "A" if it is an **adjective**.

1. direct _____
2. directory _____
3. invest _____
4. investigate _____
5. investigation _____
6. investigator _____
7. investor _____
8. reinvest _____
9. removable _____
10. remove _____

#119. Words With Prefixes & Suffixes 7

On the tree branches, write five or more words made by adding **prefixes** and/or **suffixes** to the root word.

(Tree labeled FRIEND)

#120. Words With Prefixes & Suffixes 8

Write "T" for true or "F" for false.

____ 1. **Misdirection** means to get lost.
____ 2. A **directive** is an order or command.
____ 3. A **directory** is a book of directions.
____ 4. A **director** is one who leads.
____ 5. **Directly** means soon.
____ 6. An **investigation** is a study of something.
____ 7. An **investor** is one who wears vests.
____ 8. To **investigate** means to look into something.
____ 9. **Directions** can mean points on a compass or instructions.
____ 10. An **investigator** is one who puts money into a project.

CD-404245 ©Mark Twain Media, Inc., Publishers

Language Arts Warm-Ups: Expanding Vocabulary   Root Words, Prefixes, and Suffixes

Name: _____ Date: _____

Root Words, Prefixes, and Suffixes

#121. Words With Prefixes & Suffixes 9

Match these words listed below to their meanings. The words are all based on the word **observe**. Use a dictionary if you are not sure of the definitions.

____ 1. **observance**
____ 2. **observant**
____ 3. **observation**
____ 4. **observatory**
____ 5. **observer**
____ 6. **nonobservance**

A. close study
B. the act of following laws or customs
C. failure to follow a custom
D. one who watches
E. alert, attentive
F. a place to watch the stars

#122. Words With Prefixes & Suffixes 10

Write a short definition of each word derived from the word **detect**. Use a dictionary if needed.

detect – (v) to find

1. **detection** _____
   _____

2. **detective** _____
   _____

3. **detector** _____
   _____

4. **undetectable** _____
   _____

#123. Words With Prefixes & Suffixes 11

Adding prefixes and suffixes changes the part of speech of a word. Write "N" if the word is a **noun**, "V" if it is a **verb**, or "A" if it is an **adjective**.

1. detect _____
2. detection _____
3. detector _____
4. observance _____
5. observation _____
6. observatory _____
7. observe _____
8. observer _____
9. undetectable _____
10. unobserved _____

#124. Words With Prefixes & Suffixes 12

On the tree branches, write five or more words made by adding **prefixes** and/or **suffixes** to the root word.

LOVE

Language Arts Warm-Ups: Expanding Vocabulary   Root Words, Prefixes, and Suffixes

Name: _____ Date: _____

Root Words, Prefixes, and Suffixes

#125. Root Words, Prefixes, and Suffixes Review 1

1. Write three examples of **prefixes**.
   _____

2. Write three examples of **suffixes**.
   _____

3. Write three words that include **prefixes**.
   _____
   _____

4. Write three words that include **suffixes**.
   _____
   _____

5. Write three words that include **prefixes** and **suffixes**. _____
   _____

#126. Root Words, Prefixes, and Suffixes Review 2

Write the words from the list to match the definitions.

| boldness | disorder | disrepair |
| disrespectful | fairness | quickness |

_____ 1. justice
_____ 2. daring
_____ 3. speed
_____ 4. rude
_____ 5. chaos
_____ 6. falling apart

#127. Root Words, Prefixes, and Suffixes Review 3

Match the words with their definitions.

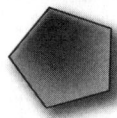

___ 1. **bilingual**   A. sad
___ 2. **disconnect**   B. truth
___ 3. **mislay**   C. a shape with four sides
___ 4. **nonfiction**
___ 5. **observant**   D. take apart
___ 6. **pentagon**   E. knowing two languages
___ 7. **quadrilateral**
___ 8. **tearful**   F. alert, attentive
                           G. a shape with five sides
                           H. lose

#128. Root Words, Prefixes, and Suffixes Review 4

On the lines, add three different prefixes to the root words. Write the new words.

1. **cover** _____
              _____
              _____

2. **lay**   _____
              _____
              _____

3. **cooked** _____
              _____
              _____

Language Arts Warm-Ups: Expanding Vocabulary   Root Words, Prefixes, and Suffixes

Name: _____ Date: _____

Root Words, Prefixes, and Suffixes

#129. Root Words, Prefixes, and Suffixes Review 5

Match the words and their definitions.

___ 1. **bicycle**
___ 2. **bimonthly**
___ 3. **decathlon**
___ 4. **discontinue**
___ 5. **harmful**
___ 6. **hexagon**
___ 7. **observatory**

A. risky
B. 10-sport Olympic event
C. a vehicle with two wheels
D. a place to watch the stars and planets
E. every two months
F. stop
G. a shape with six sides

#130. Root Words, Prefixes, and Suffixes Review 6

Match the words with their definitions.

___ 1. **biweekly**
___ 2. **boastful**
___ 3. **centennial**
___ 4. **cheerful**
___ 5. **combination**
___ 6. **continuously**
___ 7. **doubtful**
___ 8. **flavorful**

A. unsure
B. a 100-year celebration
C. every 2 weeks
D. a group of things
E. tasty
F. happy
G. proud
H. nonstop

#131. Root Words, Prefixes, and Suffixes Review 7

Add three different suffixes to the root words. Write the new words.

1. **agree** _____
   _____
   _____

2. **bold** _____
   _____
   _____

3. **like** _____
   _____
   _____

#132. Root Words, Prefixes, and Suffixes Review 8

Write the words from the list to match the definitions.

bisect   decorations   discharge
fanciful   millennium   misdeed
misshapen   nonsense   observation

1. _____ twisted
2. _____ set free
3. _____ foolishness
4. _____ crime
5. _____ 1,000 years
6. _____ ornaments
7. _____ imaginative
8. _____ cut in half
9. _____ close study

CD-404245 ©Mark Twain Media, Inc., Publishers   34

Language Arts Warm-Ups: Expanding Vocabulary   Compound Words

Name: _____   Date: _____

Compound Words

#133. Compound Words 1

A **compound word** combines two or more words to express a single idea. Circle the compound words in each sentence. Draw lines to separate the compound words into single words.

1. A cupboard made of cardboard would not be good for storing teacups and tablespoons.
2. The redhead had an outstanding workout at the football field.
3. I'll meet you in the stockroom soon. However, we cannot whitewash the staircase until this afternoon because I need a new paintbrush.

#134. Compound Words 2

Use a dictionary to write a brief definition for each compound word.

1. **copperhead** _____
_____
2. **runoff** _____
_____
3. **horsepower** _____
_____
4. **backspace** _____
_____
5. **copyright** _____
_____
6. **runway** _____
_____

#135. Compound Words 3

Whether two words should be joined to make a compound word depends on the context in the sentence. *Example:* Any bird that is blue is a blue bird, but a **bluebird** is a specific type of bird. Underline the correct word or words in each sentence.

1. Do not let the (water fall / waterfall) on the carpet.
2. We sat by a beautiful (water fall / waterfall) and watched the sunset.
3. Is (any body / anybody) welcome to join the club?
4. Is there (any body / anybody) of water nearby in which to go fishing?
5. He wore (over alls / overalls) to keep his clothes clean.
6. She spilled paint (over all / overall) the papers.

#136. Compound Words 4

Compound words are formed from components that are words on their own. For example, *haystack* is formed from the words *hay* and *stack*.

Cross out the words below that are not compound words.

dipstick

turkey

frontier

without

walrus

bypass

Language Arts Warm-Ups: Expanding Vocabulary

Compound Words

Name: _____ Date: _____

Compound Words

#137. Compound Words 5

Using the same word in each blank, make three **compound words**.

1. _____ color
2. _____ fall
3. _____ melon

Name two compound words that describe the same hot breakfast food.

4. _____
5. _____

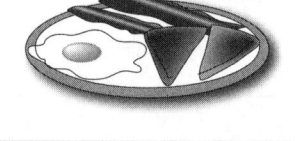

#138. Compound Words 6

How many compound words can you list that come between **pickup** and **popcorn** in the dictionary? List some of them here. Use your own paper if you need more room.

_____
_____
_____
_____
_____
_____
_____
_____
_____

#139. Compound Words 7

Write the **compound word** that fits each definition.

1. the steering bar of a bicycle

   _____

2. a small cart with one wheel used to carry garden loads

   _____

3. a short board mounted on small wheels used for cruising and performing stunts

   _____

#140. Compound Words 8

Name two titles (books, movies, comics, etc.) that contain compound words.

1. _____
2. _____

3. Circle the compound words that are spelled correctly. Rewrite the other words correctly.

   bookeeper **somewhere**
   granddaughter **newssroom**
   bluberry **cannot**

   _____
   _____
   _____

CD-404245 ©Mark Twain Media, Inc., Publishers

Language Arts Warm-Ups: Expanding Vocabulary   Compound Words

Name: _____ Date: _____

Compound Words

#141. Compound Words 9

Add *white* or *black* to the appropriate word, and then write the new compound word in the blank.

1. **wall** _____
2. **top** _____
3. **bird** _____
4. **cap** _____
5. **fish** _____
6. **berry** _____
7. **wash** _____

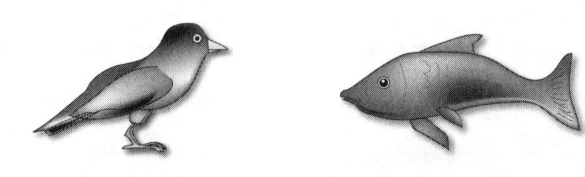

#142. Compound Words 10

Can you name three compound words that all mean **to predict** or **prophesy**?

1. _____
2. _____
3. _____

Now write a sentence using one of the words above.

4. _____
_____
_____
_____

#143. Compound Words 11

Each square contains an eight-letter compound word. Find it by starting at one of the letters and reading either clockwise or counterclockwise. Write the words in the blanks.

```
L E M
I   I
F E T
```
1. _____

```
L A C
P   E
Y N A
```
2. _____

```
N E E
A   T
G E R
```
3. _____

#144. Compound Words 12

Write a sentence using these compound words.

1. **elsewhere** _____
_____

2. **crosswalk** _____
_____

3. **scapegoat** _____
_____

Using the same word in each blank, make four compound words.

4. _____ **shoe**
5. _____ **power**
6. _____ **back**
7. _____ **fly**

CD-404245 ©Mark Twain Media, Inc., Publishers   37

Language Arts Warm-Ups: Expanding Vocabulary   Compound Words

Name: _____   Date: _____

Compound Words

#145. Compound Words 13

Four compound words have been intertwined below. Figure out how to separate each one. You will not need to change the order of the letters, just pull them apart.

Example: b r o e c d k = bedrock

1. b o g u d a r y d
   _____

2. h e l a i g d h t
   _____

3. s w a p a c l e k
   _____

4. p a b a p c e r k
   _____

#146. Compound Words 14

1. How many types of **keyboards** can you list?
   _____
   _____
   _____

2. In the kitchen, you might find a **tablespoon** and a **teaspoon**. What other non-food compound words might you find there?
   _____
   _____
   _____
   _____
   _____
   _____

#147. Compound Words 15

Match the small words to form compound names to describe places. Be sure to use all the words. Write your new words in the blanks.

1. _____
2. _____
3. _____
4. _____
5. _____
6. _____

**stand
market
ball
scraper
home
house
super
town
sky
room
grand
court**

#148. Compound Words 16

Some compounds are made of two words, such as **salad dressing**. Write a word in each blank to complete these common two-word compounds.

1. _____ cream
2. _____ school
3. polka _____
4. How many compound words begin with **tail**? Write them here.
   _____
   _____
   _____
   _____
   _____

Language Arts Warm-Ups: Expanding Vocabulary   Compound Words

Name: _____ Date: _____

Compound Words

#149. Compound Words 17

Two words have been intertwined below. Without changing the order of the letters, pull them apart into the compound word.

Example:
b r o **e c** d k = bedrock

1. s w a r o f e t _____
2. b u s c t o t t c e h r _____
3. w a p r t o e r o f _____
4. c w a h e r e l t _____
5. c o y a u r r d t _____

#150. Compound Words 18

Finish these compound words that name things you might see when you are out and about.

1. side _____
2. draw _____
3. _____ port
4. _____ pot
5. _____ pipe

#151. Compound Words 19

Many compound words join the meanings of the two words that are used. For example, **shoebox** means a **box for shoes**. List three compound words for which this is true.

1. _____
2. _____
3. _____

List three compound words for which this is **not** true.

4. _____
5. _____
6. _____

#152. Compound Words 20

Circle the compound words in the box that are spelled correctly. Rewrite the words that are incorrect.

| tomorow   becuase   together |
| anywhere   somtimes |

1. _____
2. _____
3. _____

Use one word to complete each of these compound words.

4. star _____
5. gold _____
6. jelly _____
7. _____ bowl

Language Arts Warm-Ups: Expanding Vocabulary　　　　　　　　　　　　　　　　Compound Words

Name: _____　Date: _____

Compound Words

#153. Compound Words 21

Write a compound word that means nearly the same as these compound words.

1. **sunup** _____
2. **sundown** _____
3. **aircraft** _____
4. **thoroughfare** _____

Some compound words contain hyphens. Use one of the examples in a sentence.

Examples:
mother-in-law　　African-American
old-fashioned　　blue-green

5. _____
_____
_____

#154. Compound Words 22

1. Fill in the blanks with compound words that begin with **sun**.

The sun was shining so brightly, I wore my _____. I wanted to _____, so I put on my _____. I wanted a _____, but I didn't want a _____ or _____.

Complete the names of these edible compound words.

2. horse _____
3. _____ dew
4. jelly _____
5. _____ meal

#155. Compound Words 23

Draw lines to form correct compound words that begin with either *super* or *under*.

　　　　　　natural
　　　　　　dog
super　　ground
　　　　　　mine
　　　　　　sonic
　　　　　　price
under　　hand
　　　　　　market
　　　　　　power

#156. Compound Words 24

If you were going on a camping trip, what compound words might you encounter?

1. _____
2. _____
3. _____
4. _____
5. _____
6. _____
7. _____
8. _____

On your own paper, use each of these compound words in a short sentence.

9. **watermark**　　10. **skylight**
11. **stonewall**　　12. **underhand**

Compound Words

#157. Compound Words 25

1. Change this sentence by using a compound word. Write the new sentence.

   George Clooney wrote the introductory portion of the book.

   _____
   _____
   _____

One word or two? Circle the correct form in each sentence.

3. (Everyone / Every one) is ready to go to the party.

4. (Everyone / Every one) of the costumes looks great.

#158. Compound Words 26

In how many ways can you complete this?

_____ keeper

1. _____
2. _____
3. _____
4. _____
5. _____
6. _____
7. _____
8. _____
9. _____
10. _____

#159. Compound Words 27

Find the missing links. The same missing word will be the end of one word and the beginning of another.

1. short _____ light
2. clothes _____ point
3. turtle _____ lace
4. tip _____ nail
5. text _____ keeper
6. under _____ catcher
7. fire _____ keeper
8. swim _____ case

#160. Compound Words 28

Complete these two-word compound animal names.

1. **polar** _____
2. **guinea** _____
3. **Boston** _____
4. **Tyrannosaurus** _____
5. **hermit** _____

Compound Words

#161. Compound Words 29

What one word completes all of these?

1. locker _____
2. sun _____
3. mush _____
4. _____ mate
5. ball _____

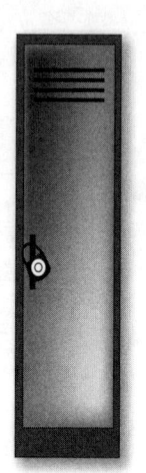

#162. Compound Words 30

Finish this story. Use at least three more compound words.

   Lisa's **cell phone** rang. It was her **girlfriend** Carmen calling. The girls had shared a **friendship** since first grade. They even lived in the same **neighborhood**. "Let's go **somewhere** tomorrow," said Carmen. So **together** they decided to

_____
_____
_____
_____
_____
_____
_____

#163. Compound Words 31

Complete these two-word place names. There may be more than one answer for some blanks.

1. Hot _____
2. Mammoth _____
3. Grand _____
4. Rocky _____

5. To illustrate **Hot Springs**, you could draw some metal springs with steam coming off of them. Think of another compound place name and illustrate it on your own paper. Show your drawing to a friend to see if he or she is able to guess the name.

#164. Compound Words 32

1. A ticket master might **undercharge** an **underage** movie-goer. Can you write a sentence with two **over** words?

_____
_____

Write either **sun** or **moon** to complete each compound word in these sentences.

2. It was such a beautiful day that Jed opened the _____ roof on his car.

3. The newlyweds went to Niagara Falls on their honey_____.

4. The rain soaked into the _____ -baked earth.

Language Arts Warm-Ups: Expanding Vocabulary   Compound Words

Name: _____ Date: _____

Compound Words

#165. Compound Words 33

1. Circle the compound words that need to be **hyphenated**.

   daughterinlaw   firstclass
   footstool   ageold
   keyboard   clockwise

2. Circle the compound words that are **adjectives**.

   downtrodden   onetime
   keystroke   up-to-date
   cargo   sunbaked

#166. Compound Words 34

Use each hyphenated compound adjective in a sentence.

1. **out-of-date** _____
   _____
2. **well-known** _____
   _____
3. **twenty-seven** _____
   _____

Write a compound word for each definition.
4. first, ahead of all others _____
5. a long, balanced plank that goes up and down when the ends are ridden
   _____
6. a board used in diving or gymnastics that helps a person jump high in the air
   _____

#167. Compound Words 35

Each square contains an eight-letter compound word. Find it by starting at one of the letters and reading either clockwise or counterclockwise. Write the words in the blanks.

```
    P O R
    R   D
    A I N
```
1. _____

```
    S I F
    H   L
    B O W
```
2. _____

```
    T E B
    O   O
    N K O
```
3. _____

#168. Compound Words 36

Circle the compound words that are written correctly. Rewrite the incorrect words.

> sons-in-law
> shoesstring
> breakthroughs
> starfishs
> musicboxs
> backpack

1. _____
2. _____
3. _____

Vocabulary

#169. Confusing Word Pairs 1

All together is a phrase meaning "everyone or everything in the same place." *Altogether* is an adverb that means "entirely, completely, or in all."

Circle **altogether** or **all together** to complete the sentences correctly.

1. I ate (altogether / all together) too much pizza last night.
2. The team sat (altogether / all together) on the bench.
3. We went to the movies (altogether / all together) as a group.
4. (Altogether / All together) we collected $150 for the charity.

#170. Confusing Word Pairs 2

Amount indicates "quantity, bulk, or mass."
Number indicates "units that can be counted."

Write **amount** or **number** on the blanks to complete these sentences correctly.

1. Can you guess the _____ of gumballs in the jar?
2. What _____ of birdseed should we buy?
3. What a huge _____ of spaghetti you ate!
4. The _____ of books I need to read for class is unbelievable.

#171. Confusing Word Pairs 3

Among is a preposition used when referring to more than two people or things.
Between is a preposition used when referring to only two people or things.

Write **between** or **among** to complete each phrase correctly.

1. _____ the two of us
2. _____ the trees of the forest
3. _____ the seven children
4. _____ the red one and the blue one
5. _____ a rock and a hard place
6. _____ all their friends

#172. Confusing Word Pairs 4

Circle the correct word to complete each sentence.

Irritate means "to cause impatience, to provoke, or to annoy."
Aggravate means "to make a condition worse."

1. When the team lost, the coach was in a state of (aggravation / irritation).
2. Scratching (aggravated / irritated) his rash.
3. My father was (aggravated / irritated) by my low grade in math.

Continual means "repeated often."
Continuous means "without a stop."

4. The (continual / continuous) sound of the surf lulls me to sleep at night.
5. The (continual / continuous) interruptions affected my concentration.

Vocabulary

#173. Confusing Word Pairs 5

Use a dictionary to write a definition for each word. On your own paper, write a sentence for each word.

1. **borrow**: _____
   _____
2. **loan**: _____
   _____
3. **fewer**: _____
   _____
4. **less**: _____
   _____

#174. Confusing Word Pairs 6

Circle the correct word in each sentence.

Effect means "to accomplish something or bring about a result."
Affect means "to act upon or influence."

1. The storm (affected / effected) our telephone service.
2. The (affect / effect) of the medication was amazing.

Accept means "to agree to something or to receive something."
Except means "to exclude or hold something apart."

3. Everyone agreed to the plan (accept / except) Herman.
4. Michael (accepted / excepted) his son's apology.

#175. Confusing Word Pairs 7

Match these words with their definitions. Feel free to use a dictionary.

___ 1. **advice**   A. A machine or instrument
___ 2. **advise**   B. To think out, plan, or invent
___ 3. **device**   C. Information provided by someone
___ 4. **devise**   D. To provide information, especially when making a decision

#176. Confusing Word Pairs 8

Good is an adjective used to modify a noun or pronoun. *Examples: We enjoy **good** food. It is **good** to see you.*

Well is an adverb that modifies verbs, adjectives, or other adverbs, or it is used as an adjective when it describes someone's health. *Examples: He looked **well**. They were **well** dressed.*

Write **good** or **well** on the blanks to complete the sentences correctly.

1. She performed _____.
2. The pizza tasted _____.
3. These peppers are _____.
4. He skates _____.
5. She made a _____ attempt to win.
6. Kent was not feeling _____.

Language Arts Warm-Ups: Expanding Vocabulary

Vocabulary

Name: _____ Date: _____

Vocabulary

#177. Homophones 1

Homophones are words that sound the same but have different meanings and spellings.

Examples: **Principal** means "a leader or chief"; "a sum of money that earns interest"; or "the most important." **Principle** means "a truth, law, or moral outlook that governs how someone behaves."

Circle the correct word to complete each sentence.
1. He was a person of strong (principles / principals).
2. The (principles / principals) of nine schools met for lunch.
3. My advice is to spend the interest, but don't touch the (principle / principal).
4. Some scientific (principles / principals) are difficult to understand.

#178. Homophones 2

Match these homophones with their definitions. Feel free to use a dictionary.

___ 1. **stationary**
___ 2. **stationery**
___ 3. **board**
___ 4. **bored**
___ 5. **bridal**
___ 6. **bridle**

A. not interested
B. paper for writing letters
C. associated with brides or weddings
D. motionless
E. leather straps used to guide a horse
F. lumber

#179. Homophones 3

Use the words listed below to complete the sentences. Feel free to use a dictionary.

| reigns   reins   straight   strait |

1. The king _____, but the queen holds the _____ of power.

2. If you travel _____ east by ship, you will reach the _____ of Gibraltar, leading to the Mediterranean Sea.

#180. Homophones 4

Use the clues and a dictionary to answer the questions using the words listed.

| pedal   peddle   residence   residents |

1. I am a place where people live. What am I? _____

2. I am part of a bicycle. What am I? _____

3. I am a verb that means to sell. What am I? _____

4. I am people who live in a specific place. What am I? _____

Language Arts Warm-Ups: Expanding Vocabulary   Vocabulary

Name: _____ Date: _____

Vocabulary

#181. Homophones 5

List the part of speech for each word and write a brief definition. Feel free to use a dictionary.

1. **cite** _____ _____
   _____
2. **site** _____ _____
   _____
3. **sight** _____ _____
   _____
4. **suite** _____ _____
   _____
5. **sweet** _____ _____
   _____

#182. Homophones 6

Match these homophones with their definitions. Feel free to use a dictionary.

___ 1. **bouillon**   A. A snack served before a meal
___ 2. **bullion**   B. A bone in the arm
___ 3. **canapé**   C. Clear liquid made from boiling meat
___ 4. **canopy**   D. Funny
___ 5. **humorous**   E. A covering to block the sun
___ 6. **humerus**   F. Gold bars

#183. Homophones 7

Circle the correct word in each sentence. Use a dictionary to check your answers.

1. If a (hoarse / horse) had a sore throat, would it sound very (hoarse / horse)?
2. If you learn this (lessen / lesson) well, it will (lessen / lesson) the study time for your test.
3. Many (patience / patients) have very little (patience / patients) when they are ill.
4. The juniors (teamed / teemed) up to play basketball against the seniors.
5. The (beach / beech) (teamed / teemed) with seashells.

#184. Homophones 8

Circle the correct word in each sentence. Write a synonym and a short definition for each circled word. Use a dictionary to check your answers.

1. The bride and groom walked hand in hand to the (altar / alter).
   _____
   _____
   _____

2. Sandy took a woodworking (coarse / course) at the Senior Center.
   _____
   _____
   _____

Language Arts Warm-Ups: Expanding Vocabulary

Vocabulary

Name: _____ Date: _____

Vocabulary

#185. Homographs 1

Homographs are words that are spelled alike but are pronounced differently and/or have different meanings. Use a dictionary to write a brief definition for the underlined word that fits the context of each sentence.

1. Darryl will **graduate** from high school in June. _____
_____

2. The **graduate** applied for several jobs last week. _____
_____

3. The woman set her groceries on the **counter**. _____
_____

4. My parents **countered** my request for a larger allowance. _____
_____

#186. Homographs 2

Use a dictionary to write a brief definition for the underlined word that fits the context of each sentence.

1. Who will **conduct** the orchestra at tonight's concert?
_____
_____

2. Water **conducts** electricity.
_____
_____

3. His **conduct** during the crisis was admirable.
_____
_____

#187. Homographs 3

Write a short definition and a sentence using each word as the part of speech listed.

1. **present** as a noun _____
_____
_____

2. **present** as a verb _____
_____
_____

3. **polish** as a verb _____
_____
_____

4. **Polish** as an adjective _____
_____

#188. Homographs 4

Sometimes the pronunciation of a homograph changes, depending on whether it is a noun or a verb. Draw a slash (/) to divide the words below into syllables. Use an accent mark (') to show which syllable of the word is stressed for the part of speech listed. Then write a short definition of the word.

1. **address** as a noun _____
_____

2. **address** as a verb _____
_____

3. **present** as a noun _____
_____

4. **present** as a verb _____
_____

Language Arts Warm-Ups: Expanding Vocabulary   Vocabulary

Name: _____ Date: _____

Vocabulary

#189. Synonyms 1

Synonyms are words that have similar meanings. Use a dictionary or thesaurus. Circle the words that are synonyms for the bold word.

1. **circumspect**
    cautious   round   prudent
2. **incidental**
    occasion   minor   significant
3. **intricate**
    complex   uncomplicated   difficult
4. **gargantuan**
    enormous   diminutive   mammoth
5. **meticulous**
    scrupulous   detailed   thorough

#190. Synonyms 2

Use a dictionary or thesaurus. Cross out the word that is not a synonym for the first word in each row.

1. **deem**   show   believe
2. **numerous**   various   one
3. **chivalrous** courteous knight
4. **delusion**   illness   mirage
5. **exclusive**   unique   similar

#191. Synonyms 3

Use a dictionary or thesaurus. Write two synonyms for each word.

1. **belligerent** _____
   _____
2. **auspicious** _____
   _____
3. **authority** _____
   _____
4. **antiquity** _____
   _____
5. **unique** _____
   _____

#192. Synonyms 4

Use a dictionary or thesaurus. Write a brief definition and a synonym for each underlined word that matches the context of the sentence.

1. The horses drank from the water **trough**. _____
   _____
   _____
2. Please, turn down the **volume**. _____
   _____
   _____
3. Can't you be more **tolerant** of your little brother? _____
   _____
   _____

Language Arts Warm-Ups: Expanding Vocabulary   Vocabulary

Name: _____ Date: _____

Vocabulary

#193. Antonyms 1

Using a dictionary or thesaurus, match the words with their antonyms. **Antonyms** are words that have opposite meanings.

___ 1. **sufficient**   A. shameful
___ 2. **completed**   B. scarce
___ 3. **complex**   C. unfinished
___ 4. **expand**   D. uncomplicated
___ 5. **glorious**   E. contract

#194. Antonyms 2

Using a dictionary or thesaurus, write an antonym and a brief definition of that antonym for each underlined word that matches the context of the sentence.

1. That plan is not very **practical**. _____
   _____

2. We are **practically** neighbors. _____
   _____

3. He took a deep breath before he began the **descent**. _____
   _____

4. Are there **sufficient** funds to cover expenses? _____
   _____

#195. Antonyms 3

Use a dictionary or thesaurus. Circle the words that are antonyms for the bold word.

1. **abundant**
   scarce   plentiful   copious
2. **odious**
   hateful   lovable   sweet
3. **monitor**
   watch   check   ignore
4. **pulchritude**
   beauty   humorous   ugliness
5. **eccentric**
   odd   unusual   normal

#196. Antonyms 4

Write two antonyms for each word. Use a dictionary or thesaurus.

1. **accelerate** _____
   _____

2. **decisive** _____
   _____

3. **marine** _____
   _____

4. **laud** _____
   _____

CD-404245 ©Mark Twain Media, Inc., Publishers   50

Vocabulary

#197. Proper Nouns and Proper Adjectives 1

Note: Always capitalize proper nouns and adjectives.

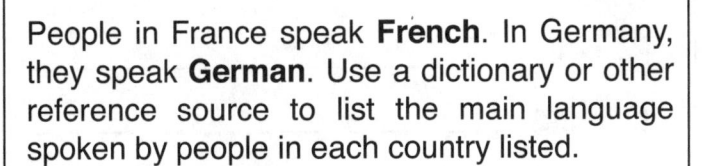

People in France speak **French**. In Germany, they speak **German**. Use a dictionary or other reference source to list the main language spoken by people in each country listed.

1. Czech Republic _____
2. Ukraine _____
3. The Netherlands _____
4. Greece _____
5. Republic of Azerbaijan _____
6. Republic of Finland _____

#198. Proper Nouns and Proper Adjectives 2

Residents of Great Britain are called **British**. People who live in Thailand are **Thai**. Use a dictionary or other reference source to list the word used for residents of each country.

1. Republic of Hungary _____
2. Republic of Lithuania _____
3. Republic of Mozambique _____
4. Republic of Zimbabwe _____

#199. Proper Nouns and Proper Adjectives 3

Use a dictionary or other reference source to find the correct spelling for each state or country.

1. Oaklahomma _____
2. Minesoda _____
3. Massashutes _____
4. Conneticut _____
5. Mississsippi _____
6. Eygpyt _____
7. Afghanistayn _____
8. Bangaladesh _____
9. Lebannon _____
10. Maylaysia _____
11. Quwait _____

#200. Proper Nouns and Proper Adjectives 4

Write two **proper nouns** for each category. Use a dictionary or other source to check the spelling.

1. U.S. cities _____
2. Presidents _____
3. Athletes _____
4. Mountain ranges _____
5. Fictional characters _____
6. Famous women _____

Language Arts Warm-Ups: Expanding Vocabulary   Vocabulary

Name: _____   Date: _____

Vocabulary

#201. Changing the Part of Speech of Words 1

Change these **nouns** to **adjectives**. Use a dictionary to check your answers.

1. beauty _____
2. fool _____
3. person _____
4. nation _____
5. style _____
6. music _____

#202. Changing the Part of Speech of Words 2

Change these **nouns** to **adverbs**. Use a dictionary to check your answers.

1. fool _____
2. child _____
3. addition _____
4. fraction _____
5. truth _____
6. whole _____

#203. Changing the Part of Speech of Words 3

Change these **verbs** to **nouns**. Use a dictionary to check your answers.

1. complicate _____
2. collide _____
3. compute _____
4. officiate _____
5. confide _____
6. patronize _____

#204. Changing the Part of Speech of Words 4

Change these **adjectives** to **adverbs**. Use a dictionary to check your answers.

1. permanent _____
2. obvious _____
3. gradual _____
4. second _____
5. practical _____
6. medical _____
7. How does changing the part of speech of words help you expand your vocabulary?
_____
_____
_____

CD-404245 ©Mark Twain Media, Inc., Publishers   52

Language Arts Warm-Ups: Expanding Vocabulary Vocabulary

Name: _____ Date: _____

Vocabulary

#205. Words From Mythology 1

Write the word for each part-human, part-animal mythological creature next to its picture. Use a dictionary or other reference source if you need help.

centaur	sphinx
minotaur	mermaid

1. _____

2. _____

3. _____

4. _____

#206. Words From Mythology 2

Use a dictionary to match these mythological creatures with their definitions.

___ 1. **satyr**   A. a tree nymph

___ 2. **basilisk**   B. a water nymph

___ 3. **dryad**   C. a reptilian creature that turned people to stone

___ 4. **naiad**

D. a creature with the head of a man and body of a goat

#207. Words From Mythology 3

Use a dictionary or other source to answer these questions.

1. What three animals were combined in a **chimera**? _____
   _____

2. What could **Pegasus** do that a normal horse could not do? _____

3. How was a **phoenix** reborn? _____
   _____
   _____

4. In what country's mythology would you find tales of **genies**? _____

5. What is an alternate spelling for **genie**?
   _____

#208. Words From Mythology 4

Use a dictionary or other source to complete the following.

1. What country is famous for **leprechauns**?
   _____

2. In which country did the gods **Ra** and **Osiris** originate? _____

3. In what country were **Vishnu**, **Brahma**, and **Shiva** honored? _____

4. When a **banshee** wailed, what did it mean?
   _____
   _____

5. An *ankh* symbolized life in ancient Egypt. Draw an ankh in the space at the right.

CD-404245 ©Mark Twain Media, Inc., Publishers

Language Arts Warm-Ups: Expanding Vocabulary

Vocabulary

Name: _____ Date: _____

Vocabulary

#209. Classifying Words 1

Circle the words from the list below that are mammals. Then pick one mammal and describe it on the lines below. Use a dictionary or other reference source to check your answers.

armadillo   earwig   echidna   halibut
javelina   moa   narwhal   ocelot
pangolin   tibia

_____
_____
_____
_____
_____
_____

#210. Classifying Words 2

Cross out the words on the list below that are <u>not</u> types of documents. Then pick one document and describe its features on the lines below. Use a dictionary to check your answers.

declaration   constitution   contract
charter   decree   honorarium
jurisdiction sinecure   statute   tenure

_____
_____
_____
_____
_____
_____
_____

#211. Classifying Words 3

Rewrite these animal names next to the correct classification. Use a dictionary or other reference source to check your answers.

manta ray   flounder   praying mantis
salamander cicada   hellbender
mud puppy   newt   earwig
halibut   walking stick
water strider   yellow-striped caecilian

Fish: _____
_____
Insects: _____
_____
Amphibians: _____
_____

#212. Classifying Words 4

Use a dictionary or other reference source to determine if each term refers to water or land. Write "W" for water or "L" for land in the blanks.

___ 1. **strait**   ___ 2. **isthmus**

___ 3. **peninsula**   ___ 4. **gulf**

___ 5. **estuary**   ___ 6. **delta**

___ 7. **fjord**   ___ 8. **billabong**

___ 9. **channel**   ___ 10. **mesa**

Language Arts Warm-Ups: Expanding Vocabulary   Vocabulary

Name: _____ Date: _____

Vocabulary

#213. Classifying Words 5

Match the words from the list to the definitions. Use a dictionary to check your answers.

A. **ichthyologist**   B. **aviary**
C. **herpetologist**   D. **apiary**
E. **entomologist**

1. You would find many birds here: _____
2. The insects that live here make lots of honey: _____
3. A specialist in reptiles and amphibians: _____
4. One who specializes in the study of fish: _____
5. One who studies insects: _____

#214. Classifying Words 6

Cross out the words on the list that are <u>not</u> birds. Then pick one bird and describe it on the lines below. Use a dictionary or other reference source to check your answers.

barracuda   yellow jacket   emu   kiwi
fibula   finch   kookaburra
quetzal   egret   marlin

_____
_____
_____
_____
_____
_____

#215. Classifying Words 7

Use a dictionary to match these types of doctors with their specialties.

___ 1. **dermatologist**   A. eyes
___ 2. **obstetrician**   B. young children
___ 3. **oncologist**
___ 4. **pediatrician**   C. delivering babies
___ 5. **neurologist**
___ 6. **ophthalmologist**   D. nervous system
                              E. cancer
                              F. skin

#216. Classifying Words 8

Use a dictionary to write a brief definition for each math term. Be sure to use the mathematical definitions.

1. **octothorpe**: _____
_____
2. **radical**: _____
_____
3. **googol**: _____
_____
4. **hexagram**: _____
_____
5. **octahedron**: _____
_____
6. **protractor**: _____
_____

CD-404245 ©Mark Twain Media, Inc., Publishers

Language Arts Warm-Ups: Expanding Vocabulary   Vocabulary

Name: _____   Date: _____

Vocabulary

#217. Foreign Words and Phrases 1

Some foreign words are used in English without a change in spelling or meaning. Use a dictionary to write a short definition below for these German words also commonly used in English.

1. **verboten**: _____
   _____

2. **sauerkraut**: _____
   _____

3. **doppelganger**: _____
   _____

4. **kindergarten**: _____
   _____

5. **gesundheit**: _____
   _____

#218. Foreign Words and Phrases 2

Use a dictionary to match these Spanish words commonly used in English with their definitions.

___ 1. **sombrero**   A. an enthusiastic person

___ 2. **siesta**   B. a flour tortilla wrapped around meat, beans, or cheese

___ 3. **burrito**

___ 4. **salsa**   C. an afternoon nap
                         D. a spicy sauce

___ 5. **aficionado**   E. a large-brimmed hat for blocking the sun

#219. Foreign Words and Phrases 3

Use a dictionary to answer the questions, and then on your own paper, use each phrase in a sentence.

1. What does the Spanish phrase **mano a mano** mean? _____
   _____

2. What does the Italian phrase **dolce vita** mean? _____
   _____

3. What does the Greek phrase **hoi polloi** mean? _____
   _____

#220. Foreign Words and Phrases 4

British English and **American English** sometimes seem like two different languages. Write the letter of the American English word from the list to match the British English word. Use a dictionary if you get confused.

British   American

___ 1. **anorak**   A. **clothespin**

___ 2. **tram**   B. **parka**

___ 3. **clothes peg**   C. **underpass**

___ 4. **lift**   D. **streetcar**

___ 5. **sorbet**   E. **sherbet**

___ 6. **subway**   F. **elevator**

Language Arts Warm-Ups: Expanding Vocabulary   Vocabulary

Name: _____   Date: _____

Vocabulary

#221. Foreign Words and Phrases 5

Many English words use Greek root words. For example, *anthrop* means "human." *Anthropologist, misanthrope,* and *philanthropy* are English words using *anthrop* as a root word. Use a dictionary to find the definition for these words using the Greek *chron,* meaning "time."

1. **chronicle**: _____
   _____

2. **chronic**: _____
   _____

3. **chronograph**: _____
   _____

4. **synchronize**: _____
   _____

#222. Foreign Words and Phrases 6

On your own paper, write a sentence using each of these French phrases. Use a dictionary or other source for clarification if needed.

1. coup de grâce   2. faux pas
3. nom de plume   4. savoir-faire
5. carte blanche   6. enfant terrible
7. cause célèbre   8. de rigueur
9. fait accompli   10. je ne sais quoi
11. carte blanche

#223. Latin Phrases 1

Many English words come from Latin. For example, *dict* means "**to say**." **Predict**, **contradict**, and **edict** are common English words using *dict* as a root word. Use a dictionary to write five or more English words for each Latin root word.

1. *port* - to carry _____
   _____

2. *scrib* or *script* - to write _____
   _____

3. *ject* - to throw _____
   _____

4. *vert* - to turn _____
   _____

#224. Latin Phrases 2

Use a dictionary or other source to match these Latin phrases with their meanings.

___ 1. *casus belli*   A. an act of
___ 2. *caveat emptor*   the gods
___ 3. *deus ex machina*   B. after the fact
___ 4. *ecce homo*   C. the cause
___ 5. *ex post facto*   of a war
                            D. let the buyer
                               beware
                            E. behold the
                               man

CD-404245 ©Mark Twain Media, Inc., Publishers

Language Arts Warm-Ups: Expanding Vocabulary   Vocabulary

Name: _____   Date: _____

Vocabulary

#225. Latin Phrases 3

Read the translations for these Latin phrases used in English. On your own paper, write sentences using each phrase correctly. Use a dictionary if needed.

1. *ad absurdum* - to the point of absurdity
2. *ad infinitum* - to infinity
3. *ad nauseam* - to a sickening degree
4. *bona fide* - in good faith; genuine
5. *carpe diem* - seize the day

#226. Latin Phrases 4

Use a dictionary or other reference source to answer these questions.

1. How much does a lawyer charge if she works **pro bono**? _____
   _____

2. Would you want to be a **persona non grata**? Why or why not? _____
   _____
   _____

3. Why were sailors terrified about sailing to **terra incognita**? _____
   _____
   _____

#227. Latin Phrases 5

Use a dictionary or other source to find the meanings of these Latin phrases, and then on your own paper, use them in a sentence.

1. *mea culpa*: _____
   _____
   _____

2. *quid pro quo*: _____
   _____
   _____

3. *veni, vidi, vici*: _____
   _____
   _____

#228. Latin Phrases 6

Underline the Latin phrase in each sentence. Rewrite the phrase in English so that it fits smoothly in the sentence. Use a dictionary to check your answers.

1. While her mother was on vacation, Amy's grandmother acted **in loco parentis**.
   _____
   _____

2. "I can't stop now," Maria shouted, "I am **in medias res**!"
   _____

3. The archaeologist found the pottery **in situ**.
   _____

Language Arts Warm-Ups: Expanding Vocabulary

Figurative Language

Name: _____ Date: _____

Figurative Language

#229. Idioms 1

Idioms are commonly used expressions that mean something different from the actual words. For example, **"Don't bite off more than you can chew"** has nothing to do with eating. It means not to try something that's too difficult or advanced.

Underline the idiom in each sentence.
1. "No, I won't cheat on the test," Sara said. "It goes against my grain."
2. Jeremy was on cloud nine after he passed his vocabulary test.
3. Heather tried to knit a sweater, but she was all thumbs.
4. If you can't cut the mustard at practice, you won't make the team.

#230. Idioms 2

1. What does **"I'm going to hit the hay"** mean? Check the correct choice.

   _____ I'm going to practice boxing.
   _____ I'm going to clean out the barn.
   _____ I'm going to bed.

2. **"It's raining cats and dogs"** is a common idiom. On your own paper, draw one picture showing the literal meaning of the saying and one picture showing the actual meaning of the saying.

#231. Idioms 3

1. Before she gave her speech in class, Tanya **had butterflies in her stomach**. This sentence means (check the best answer):
   _____ Tanya had eaten a caterpillar.
   _____ Tanya was so nervous that her stomach felt fluttery.
   _____ Tanya had a serious disease.

2. Which of the following idioms means "to work late into the night"? Check the best choice.
   _____ burn the candle at both ends
   _____ burn the midnight oil
   _____ burn your bridges

#232. Idioms 4

Check all the idioms below that mean **grumpy**.

_____ 1. cold turkey
_____ 2. got up on the wrong side of the bed
_____ 3. faced the music
_____ 4. has a bee in her bonnet
_____ 5. has his dander up
_____ 6. knows the ropes

CD-404245 ©Mark Twain Media, Inc., Publishers

Figurative Language

#233. Idioms 5

1. If you **rule the roost**, you (check the best answer):

    ___ have to clean out the chicken coop.

    ___ have to gather eggs.

    ___ are the boss.

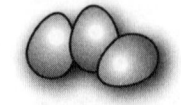

2. If someone says, "**I've got a bone to pick with you**," you should (check the best answer):

    ___ ask what's wrong.

    ___ say "Thank you."

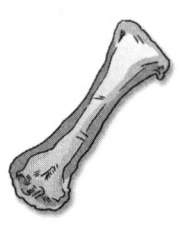

    ___ eat with the person.

#234. Idioms 6

Use context clues to determine the meaning of each underlined idiom.

1. You can have anything you want for your birthday. The **sky is the limit**!
   _____
   _____

2. I can't understand our language arts assignment. **It's Greek to me**.
   _____
   _____

3. If you'd finish your term paper early, you wouldn't have to stay up all night and **burn the midnight oil**.
   _____
   _____

#235. Idioms 7

Match the two idioms that have similar meanings.

___ 1. **haste makes waste**

___ 2. **all bark and no bite**

___ 3. **down in the dumps**

___ 4. **a shot in the dark**

___ 5. **between a rock and a hard place**

   A. **a real pussycat**

   B. **out of the frying pan and into the fire**

   C. **when pigs fly**

   D. **Rome wasn't built in a day**

   E. **feeling blue**

#236. Idioms 8

Write the meaning of each idiom in your own words.

1. **a slip of the tongue** _____
   _____

2. **elbow grease** _____
   _____

3. **shake a leg** _____
   _____

4. **put your best foot forward** _____
   _____

5. **in over your head** _____
   _____

Language Arts Warm-Ups: Expanding Vocabulary   Figurative Language

Name: _____   Date: _____

Figurative Language

#237. Imagery 1

Imagery (IM-uj-ree) uses words to paint a picture in the reader's mind.

On your own paper, write a description of this scene, painting a picture with words.

#238. Imagery 2

1. **Imagery** describes sounds to interest readers. Write four **sound** words.
   _____
   _____

2. **Imagery** describes smells to interest readers. Write four **scent** words.
   _____
   _____

3. **Imagery** describes tastes to interest readers. Write four **taste** words.
   _____
   _____

#239. Imagery 3

Imagery describes sights, sounds, scents, tastes, and textures to paint a word picture. Underline the words in the paragraph below that describe the five senses: **sight, sound, smell, taste,** and **touch**.

    I opened one eye when my alarm clock buzzed. My room was still dark, but I could smell coffee. When the scent of sizzling bacon hit my nose, my mouth watered and my stomach growled. I knew Mom would cook it until it was crunchy, just the way I like it. My feet met the cold, hard floor as I got out of bed. I threw on my soft, red sweatshirt and jeans and headed for breakfast.

#240. Imagery 4

Imagery describes how things feel so readers can imagine the experience. Draw lines between the words that describe a feeling and the thing they describe.

1. **scratchy**   A. wool sweater
2. **nubby**   B. angora fur
3. **silky**   C. pillow
4. **rough**   D. carpet
5. **soft**   E. sandpaper

CD-404245 ©Mark Twain Media, Inc., Publishers   61

Language Arts Warm-Ups: Expanding Vocabulary Figurative Language

Name: _____ Date: _____

Figurative Language

#241. Imagery 5

How does each of the following feel when you touch it? Write a touch word for each.

1. **sidewalk** _____
2. **grass** _____
3. **ice cream** _____
4. **water** _____
5. **tree trunk** _____

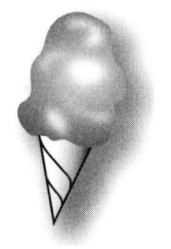

#242. Imagery 6

Imagery uses specific words to paint an accurate picture. For example, using *Irish Setter* instead of *dog* tells the reader 'what kind of dog.' Write a specific word for the general ones below.

1. **cereal** _____
2. **flower** _____
3. **person** _____
4. **shoes** _____
5. **music** _____

#243. Imagery 7

1. Circle the words that are specific.

   ocean   basketball   sport
   cottonwood   movie

2. **Imagery** uses **details** to make something stand out. Write the unique detail about each mug beneath it.

#244. Imagery 8

Fill in each blank with a specific word. A general hint is given.

The (boy) _____ visited the (mountains) _____ with his (family) _____. They caught (fish) _____ in the (creek) _____ and cooked them for (a meal) _____.

Figurative Language

#245. Imagery 9

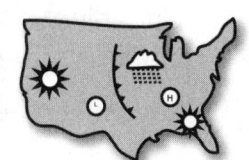

Describe today's weather. Remember to use **imagery** and as many of the five senses (**sight, sound, smell, taste, touch**) as you can.

_____
_____
_____
_____
_____
_____
_____

#246. Imagery 10

1. Circle the words that describe **sounds**.

   cry   dirt   fell   brown
   bark   thud   tap   clomp
   cheese   clap   metallic   whimper

2. Circle the words that describe **textures** (**touch**).

   red   smooth   rough   spicy
   hard   lemony   sharp   large
   shiny   crusty   tangy   sticky

#247. Imagery 11

Onomatopoeia (ON-uh-MAH-tuh-PEE-uh) means "a word that sounds like what it is." Two examples are *buzz* and *zoom*. Think of five more and write them below.

1. _____
2. _____
3. _____
4. _____
5. _____

Buzz 
Buzz

#248. Imagery 12

1. Circle the words that describe **taste**.

   spicy   hard   blue   sweet
   peppery   sour   noisy   bland
   blunt   fruity   itchy   cloudy

2. With **imagery**, write sentences that describe a slice of pizza to someone who cannot see.

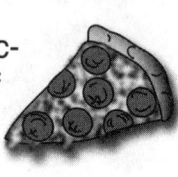

_____
_____
_____
_____
_____

Language Arts Warm-Ups: Expanding Vocabulary   Figurative Language

Name: _____ Date: _____

Figurative Language

#249. Simile 1

A **simile** (SIM-uh-lee) compares two unlike things using the words *like* or *as*.

1. What two things are being compared in this sentence?

    The girl laughed like a hyena.
    _____
    _____

2. Finish this sentence with a **simile**.

    Going to the dentist is like _____
    _____
    _____

#250. Simile 2

1. Underline the sentence below that is a **simile**.

    Love is a rose.   Love is like a rose.

2. What do these similes mean?

    March comes in like a lion and goes out like a lamb.
    _____
    _____
    _____

3. Write your own simile by filling in the blank.
    _____
    _____
    as the wind.

#251. Simile 3

1. Underline the sentence below that contains a **simile**.

    My dog smells like gym socks.

    My dog smells his dinner.

2. Write your own **simile** by completing the sentence.

    _____
    _____
    smells like a wet dog.

#252. Simile 4

1. Write three similes using the word *like*.
    _____
    _____
    _____
    _____
    _____

2. Write three similes using the word *as*.
    _____
    _____
    _____
    _____
    _____
    _____

Language Arts Warm-Ups: Expanding Vocabulary   Figurative Language

Name: _____   Date: _____

Figurative Language

#253. Simile 5

Imagine you must explain "sky" to someone who has never seen it. Write a short description on these lines.

"The sky is like…" _____
_____
_____
_____
_____
_____
_____
_____

#254. Simile 6

Many similes use comparisons to animals. Draw lines to connect the trait to the animal.

1. Sly as   A. a lamb
2. Quiet as   B. an owl
3 Gentle as   C. a fox
4. Wise as   D. a mouse

#255. Simile 7

1. Use at least two of the words below to create an appropriate **simile**. Write it below.

   jeans   happiness   heart   snail
   flower   pizza   peace   ring

   _____
   _____

2. How is the following **simile** true? Think of as many ways as you can.

   A race car is like an athlete.

   _____
   _____
   _____

#256. Simile 8

1. Underline the **simile** below.

   A rainbow is a prism.

   A rainbow is like a box of crayons.

2. Complete the following sentence.

   My pet dinosaur is like _____
   _____,

   because _____
   _____.

CD-404245 ©Mark Twain Media, Inc., Publishers   65

Figurative Language

#257. Metaphor 1

A **metaphor** (MET-uh-for) compares two unlike things directly, without using *like* or *as*.

1. Underline the sentence below that is a metaphor.

    Love is a rose.   Love is like a rose.

2. In the metaphor below, what two things are being compared, and what does the comparison mean?

    I can't go to the movie tonight. I'm under an avalanche of homework.

    _____
    _____
    _____

#258. Metaphor 2

Read the poem by Carl Sandburg entitled, "Fog."

> The fog comes
> on little cat feet.
>
> It sits looking
> over harbor and city
> on silent haunches
> and then moves on.

In what ways is fog like a cat?

_____
_____
_____
_____

#259. Metaphor 3

1. What is being compared in the **metaphor** below? What does it mean?

    Has your train of thought jumped its track?

    _____

    _____ is compared to _____.

    This means _____
    _____

2. Ann's mom called Ann the "Birthday Queen."

    Is Ann royalty?
    Circle one: Yes   No

    What does Ann's mom mean? _____
    _____
    _____

#260. Metaphor 4

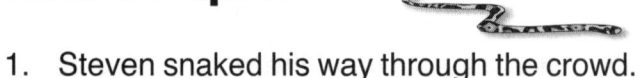

1. Steven snaked his way through the crowd. What is being compared?

    _____
    _____
    _____

2. Write a metaphor comparing a weather condition to an animal.

    _____
    _____
    _____

    In what ways is this true?

    _____
    _____
    _____

Language Arts Warm-Ups: Expanding Vocabulary   Figurative Language

Name: _____   Date: _____

Figurative Language

#261. Metaphor 5

1. Write a **metaphor** describing someone who is angry.

   _____
   _____
   _____

2. This is true because _____
   _____
   _____
   _____
   _____

#262. Metaphor 6

The sentences below mean almost the same thing. The difference is in the effect each sentence has on the reader. Describe the differences below. (Hint: how do you react to each sentence's comparison?)

   Love is a rose.
   Love is like a rose.

_____
_____
_____
_____
_____
_____

#263. Metaphor 7

Look for three **metaphors**. They could be anywhere—newspapers, textbooks, library books, magazines, blogs—anywhere there's print! Write them below and tell where you found them:

1. _____
   _____

2. _____
   _____
   _____

3. _____
   _____

#264. Metaphor 8

1. "My classroom is an oven" means (check the correct choice)

   ____ My classroom contains ovens.

   ____ My classroom is hot.

   ____ My classroom is for baking.

2. Fill in the blank with your own **metaphor**.

   The school cafeteria is _____
   _____
   _____.

   In what ways is this true? _____
   _____
   _____

CD-404245 ©Mark Twain Media, Inc., Publishers   67

Language Arts Warm-Ups: Expanding Vocabulary

Figurative Language

Name: _____ Date: _____

Figurative Language

#265. Adage 1

An **adage** (ADD-uj) is an old, wise saying containing universal truth. Many adages are also metaphors.

Let sleeping dogs lie is not really about dogs. What does the adage mean?

_____
_____
_____
_____
_____

#266. Adage 2

Check the sentence below that most closely shows the meaning of the adage.

Don't bite the hand that feeds you.

____ Don't bite your mother.
____ Be good to those who provide for you.
____ Be careful when you eat.

Can you think of another adage that has a similar meaning?

_____
_____
_____

#267. Adage 3

1. Some adages can be modernized. **A watched pot never boils** is an old adage. Write a modern version by completing the following sentence:

   A listened-for cell phone never _____.

2. Imagine you are working on a class project with a group. How might this adage apply?

   Too many cooks spoil the broth.

   _____
   _____
   _____

#268. Adage 4

1. **Nothing ventured, nothing gained** is closest in meaning to which other adage listed below? Check the best answer.

   ____ Use it or lose it.
   ____ No pain, no gain.
   ____ Where there's a will, there's a way.

2. What do these adages mean?

   _____
   _____
   _____
   _____
   _____

Language Arts Warm-Ups: Expanding Vocabulary   Figurative Language

Name: _____ Date: _____

Figurative Language

#269. Adage 5

1. "I can't tell you. I have to show you." This best tells the meaning of which adage? Check the correct one below.

    ____ All's fair in love and war.

    ____ Beauty is in the eye of the beholder.

    ____ A picture is worth a thousand words.

2. **All work and no play makes Jack a dull boy** emphasizes the importance of (check the best answer)

    ____ work.

    ____ brains.

    ____ play.

#270. Adage 6

These two adages have the opposite meaning. Which one do you think is true? Why?

Absence makes the heart grow fonder.

Out of sight, out of mind.

_____
_____
_____
_____
_____
_____
_____
_____

#271. Adage 7

1. "Early to bed, early to rise, makes a man healthy, wealthy, and wise."
Write your own version of this adage:

    Early to bed, early to rise, makes a person _____
    _____
    _____

2. How can this adage be true? **Whether you think you can or you think you can't, you're right.**
    _____
    _____
    _____
    _____

#272. Adage 8

The grass is always greener on the other side of the fence is closest in meaning to which of the following? Check the correct one.

    ____ Cows would rather be in a pasture other than their own.

    ____ The neighbors take better care of their lawn than you do.

    ____ People always think someone else is better off than they are.

How else could you phrase this adage?

_____
_____
_____
_____

CD-404245 ©Mark Twain Media, Inc., Publishers   69

Language Arts Warm-Ups: Expanding Vocabulary   Figurative Language

Name: _____ Date: _____

Figurative Language

#273. Cliché 1

A **cliché** (klee-SHAY) is a saying that's so common it's no longer interesting. Many metaphors, similes, adages, and idioms are clichés.

1. Finish this cliché:

   stubborn as a _____

Good writers try to avoid clichés and write something fresh and original.

2. **Quiet as a mouse** is a cliché. Write a simile that is not a cliché.

   Quiet as _____

#274. Cliché 2

1. Some clichés don't make sense. For example, *happy as a clam*. How happy IS a clam, anyway?

   _____
   _____
   _____

2. Write an original simile that is more accurate than *happy as a clam*.

   Happy as _____
   _____
   _____

#275. Cliché 3

1. These two clichés have similar meanings: *like a fish out of water* and *like a square peg in a round hole*. What do these clichés mean?

   _____
   _____
   _____

2. **Cool as a cucumber** is a cliché. Think of 3 original endings and write them below.

   Cool as _____.

   Cool as _____.

   Cool as _____.

#276. Cliché 4

1. If a friend says, "*I slept like a log*," is that good? Why or why not?

   _____
   _____
   _____
   _____

2. **Slick as a whistle** is a cliché. Write its meaning below.

   _____
   _____
   _____
   _____

CD-404245 ©Mark Twain Media, Inc., Publishers

Language Arts Warm-Ups: Expanding Vocabulary   Figurative Language

Name: _____ Date: _____

Figurative Language

#277. Cliché 5

1. **Smooth as glass** and **smooth as silk** are similar clichés. Which do you think is more accurate and why?
   _____
   _____
   _____

2. **Easy as pie** is a cliché that means a task is simple. Look up the steps for making a pie. Does this look easy to you? Why or why not?
   _____
   _____
   _____
   _____

#278. Cliché 6

1. **Skinny as a rail** means that someone is very thin. From what you can find out about rails, is this description true? Why or why not?
   _____
   _____
   _____

2. **Like greased lightning** is a cliché meaning really fast. Look up the speed of light. How fast is lightning?
   _____
   _____
   _____

#279. Cliché 7

1. "I'll have your order out in a jiffy," the cafe server said. **In a jiffy** is a cliché. What original phrase or standard English could the server have said to mean the same thing?
   _____
   _____
   _____

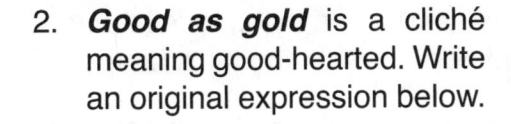

2. **Good as gold** is a cliché meaning good-hearted. Write an original expression below.

   Good as _____
   _____
   _____

#280. Cliché 8

1. The coach's face was red as a beet as he shouted at his losing team. Write an original sentence below that shows the coach's anger without clichés.
   _____
   _____
   _____
   _____

2. **Red as a beet** is a cliché that could show several conditions. List three possibilities below.
   _____
   _____
   _____
   _____

CD-404245 ©Mark Twain Media, Inc., Publishers

Language Arts Warm-Ups: Expanding Vocabulary

Figurative Language

Name: _____ Date: _____

Figurative Language

#281. Personificiation 1

Personification (pur-SAWN-i-fi-KA-shun) is figurative language that gives human traits to non-human things.

The old truck coughed and sputtered.

What is the non-human thing in this example?

1. _____

Which two words are things that humans do?

2. _____

3. _____

#282. Personificiation 2

Underline the **personification** in these sentences, then rewrite each sentence without using personification.

1. The sun smiled down on the hikers.
   _____
   _____

2. The cruel mirror showed the person's every flaw.
   _____
   _____
   _____
   _____

#283. Personificiation 3

Underline the **personification** in these sentences, then rewrite each sentence without using personification.

1. The star I wished on winked at me.
   _____
   _____
   _____

2. The trout danced in the stream.
   _____
   _____
   _____
   _____

#284. Personificiation 4

1. Put a check beside the sentence that best shows **personification**.

   ___ The ocean waved.

   ___ The ocean waved goodbye.

2. Based on your choice above, what do you think the author was trying to tell the reader? Write down what you think happened.
   _____
   _____
   _____
   _____

Language Arts Warm-Ups: Expanding Vocabulary　　　　　　　　Figurative Language

Name: _____ Date: _____

Figurative Language

#285. Personificiation 5

1. Fill in the blank to **personify** the chair in the sentence below.

   The desk chair _____ _____ when the student dumped a pile of books on it.

2. Fill in the blank to **personify** the acorn in the sentence below.

   The acorn _____ of becoming big and mighty.

#286. Personificiation 6

Complete the sentences below.

1. The mountain remembers _____ _____ _____ _____ _____

2. The moon teaches _____ _____ _____ _____ _____

#287. Personificiation 7

Put a check beside the sentence that shows **personification**.

___ The cactus blooms in the spring.

___ The cactus brings us blooms in the spring.

#288. Personificiation 8

Write a sentence with **personification** using these two words:

　　　rock　　　**wept**

_____
_____
_____
_____
_____
_____
_____

CD-404245 ©Mark Twain Media, Inc., Publishers　　73

Language Arts Warm-Ups: Expanding Vocabulary Figurative Language

Name: _____ Date: _____

Figurative Language

#289. Allusion 1

An **allusion** (uh-LOOZH-un) is a reference to something well known in literature or history.

1. "I don't like to hang around with Michael. He's such an Eeyore."
   Eeyore is an allusion to what stories? _____
   What does the sentence say about Michael's outlook on life? _____
   _____

2. "Behave," the babysitter said, "or I'll send my flying monkeys after you!"
   Flying monkeys is an allusion to what story? _____
   _____

#290. Allusion 2

1. "She barged in like Goldilocks." What does this **allusion** to the story "The Three Bears" mean?
   _____
   _____
   _____

2. When the twins' mother came home and saw the mess, she said, "I suppose you're going to blame the Cat in the Hat." What does this **allusion** mean?
   _____
   _____
   _____
   _____

#291. Allusion 3

1. "She found those lost gloves so quickly, she must be Nancy Drew!" Put a check beside the statement that best describes the **allusion**.
   ___ She is a magician.
   ___ She is a detective.
   ___ She is a store clerk.

2. "He may be 56 years old, but he's a real Peter Pan." Put a check beside the statement that best describes the **allusion**.
   ___ He can fly.
   ___ He leads a gang.
   ___ He acts like a boy.

#292. Allusion 4

1. Put a check beside the word that best completes the sentence: If someone's hair is like Rapunzel's, it is
   ___ red.
   ___ long.
   ___ curly.

2. The term "Cinderella story" is a **clichéd allusion** to the fairy tale. Put a check beside the best meaning for that allusion.
   ___ A fairy godmother helps someone.
   ___ Someone goes to a party and meets royalty.
   ___ Someone from a lowly background becomes highly successful.

CD-404245 ©Mark Twain Media, Inc., Publishers

Language Arts Warm-Ups: Expanding Vocabulary   Figurative Language

Name: _____ Date: _____

Figurative Language

#293. Allusion 5

1. "She is such a Grinch, she won't let us have a class party."
   "She won't let us have a party. She's a Tin Man who needs a trip to Oz."

   The main idea of these sentences is similar. What is it? _____
   _____
   _____

2.  When the group was done roasting marshmallows, Jason put out the campfire. "Smokey would be proud," the camp leader said.

   Who is Smokey? _____
   _____

#294. Allusion 6

Check the **allusion** or explanation that best completes these sentences.

1. My kitten's name is Curious George because
   ____ he eats bananas.
   ____ he came here on a ship.
   ____ he gets into everything.

2. When Marissa won the beauty pageant, she knew she was no longer
   ____ Raggedy Ann.
   ____ Sleeping Beauty.
   ____ the Ugly Duckling.

#295. Symbolism 1

A **symbol** (SIM-bul) is figurative language in which a concrete thing is meant to represent an abstract idea or larger concept. For example, one symbol of the United States is the flag.

1. What is another **symbol** for the United States?
   _____
   _____

2.  Sometimes authors use **spring** to symbolize youth. If that is so, then what would **winter** symbolize?
   _____

#296. Symbolism 2

Check the best answer.

1. Which of the birds listed below is used to symbolize wisdom? 
   ____ loon
   ____ owl
   ____ eagle

2. Which of the following best symbolizes education?
   ____ a diploma
   ____ a sports team
   ____ a book

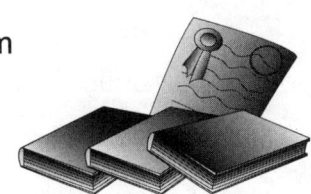

CD-404245 ©Mark Twain Media, Inc., Publishers

Language Arts Warm-Ups: Expanding Vocabulary

Figurative Language

Name: _____ Date: _____

Figurative Language

#297. Symbolism 3

Check the best answer.

1. Which of the following birds is often used to symbolize war?

    ___ hawk

    ___ turkey

    ___ vulture

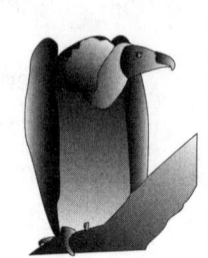

2. Which of the birds listed below is used to symbolize peace?

    ___ swallow

    ___ robin

    ___ dove

#298. Symbolism 4

Colors are often used as **symbols**. Their meanings may be different in different cultures. Check the best answer.

1. Which color is often used to symbolize life?

    ___ pink

    ___ brown

    ___ green

2. When we say that someone feels blue, blue symbolizes:

    ___ fear.

    ___ sadness.

    ___ anger.

#299. Symbolism 5

Check the best answer.

1. In literature, a river is often used to symbolize the journey of life. Which of the following could also be used?

    ___ a jet

    ___ a cloud

    ___ a road

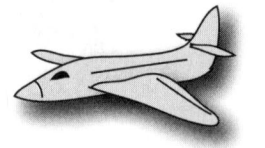

2. Which of the following could a circle symbolize?

    ___ eternity

    ___ peace

    ___ death

#300. Symbolism 6

1. Write a statement using **fire** as a symbol for a larger, abstract idea.

    _____
    _____
    _____

2. Write a statement using **night** as a symbol for a larger, abstract idea.

    _____
    _____
    _____

3. Think of a symbol for **hope**, and use it in a sentence below.

    _____
    _____
    _____

CD-404245 ©Mark Twain Media, Inc., Publishers

Language Arts Warm-Ups: Expanding Vocabulary   Figurative Language

Name: _____   Date: _____

Figurative Language

#301. Hyperbole 1

Hyperbole (high-PER-bol-ee) is figurative language that uses **exaggeration**. Check the best choice.

1. I've told you _____ times to pick up your clothes.
   - ___ two
   - ___ a hundred
   - ___ a million

2. "I spent a month there one week." This hyperbole describes a place that is:
   - ___ exciting.
   - ___ busy.
   - ___ dull.

#302. Hyperbole 2

Hyperbole is often used in humor. Use hyperbole to complete the following:

1. The test was so hard that _____

2. The town was so small _____

3. The movie was so bad _____

4. The car was so fast _____

#303. Hyperbole 3

Use **hyperbole** to complete the following.

1. The sky was so blue _____

2. The weather was so cold _____

3. My dog is so smart _____

#304. Hyperbole 4

1. Use **hyperbole** to complete the following. The food was so overcooked _____

2. "The shot heard 'round the world" refers to the beginning of the American Revolutionary War. Why is this hyperbole? _____

3. "Time stood still." Why is this hyperbole? _____

Figurative Language

#305. Hyperbole 5

Check the phrase with the correct meaning.

1. "His eyes shot daggers" is hyperbole describing someone's eyes.
   ___ He had trick eyeglasses on.
   ___ He was a spy.
   ___ His eyes gave a violent look.

2. "The woman's high voice shattered glass." This hyperbole means that the woman's voice was:
   ___ strong.
   ___ weak.
   ___ untrained.

#306. Hyperbole 6

Check the word below that best describes the statements.

1. "That was the longest day of my life" is hyperbole about what kind of day?
   ___ fun
   ___ sad
   ___ boring

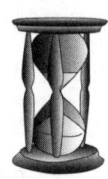

2. "You could fry an egg on the sidewalk" is hyperbole about what kind of weather?
   ___ balmy
   ___ cold
   ___ hot

#307. Hyperbole 7

For each numbered item, match two of the hyperbole fragments to make a complete sentence.

___ 1. If I've told you once,
___ 2. These math problems are so hard,
___ 3 I want to win the game so bad,
___ 4. She's so mean,

   A. even Einstein couldn't do them.
   B. she even makes Cruella De Vil look good.
   C. I've told you a thousand times.
   D. I can taste it.

#308. Hyperbole 8

Use hyperbole to complete the following statements.

1. The movie was so good _____

2. The sunset was so beautiful _____

3. The gym shoes cost so much _____

Language Arts Warm-Ups: Expanding Vocabulary   Figurative Language

Name: _____ Date: _____

Figurative Language

#309. Synecdoche 1

Synecdoche (suh-NEK-duh-kee) is figurative language in which a part is mentioned for the whole or a whole is mentioned for a part.

1. "Man, look at those cool wheels." Check the word that best shows the meaning of *wheels*.

   ____ wheels
   ____ tires
   ____ car

2. "The crown imposed new taxes." Check the word that best shows the meaning of *crown*.

   ____ head
   ____ king or queen
   ____ something worn on the head

#310. Synecdoche 2

1. "The hands will clean up when we're done." Check the word that best shows the meaning of **hands**.

   ____ hands
   ____ gloves
   ____ workers

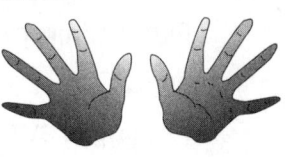

2. If someone said, "Look at those fancy threads!" how should you reply?

   ____ "Quit insulting me."
   ____ "Where?"
   ____ "Thank you."

   Threads means _____.

#311. Synecdoche 3

1. "The law arrested the man for stealing." Check the choice to which **The law** refers.

   ____ the police officer
   ____ the lawyer
   ____ the judge

2. "Where've you been, cowboy? I just herded 50 head into the high country." **Head** refers to:

   ____ cattle.
   ____ brains.
   ____ aces.

#312. Synecdoche 4

1. At dinner time, Grandma told Grandpa to come to the table for their daily bread. **Bread** means:

   ____ money.
   ____ dinner.
   ____ a loaf of bread.

2. "The tap dancers pounded the boards." In this sentence, **boards** means (check the best answer):

   ____ the stage.
   ____ wooden planks.
   ____ a hard test.

79

Language Arts Warm-Ups: Expanding Vocabulary

Dictionary Skills

Name: _____ Date: _____

Dictionary Skills

#313. Using a Dictionary/Thesaurus 1

Write "D" for **dictionary** or "T" for **thesaurus** to indicate which would be better to use for each task.

___ 1. Determining the part of speech of a word
___ 2. Finding a synonym for a word
___ 3. Finding the exact definition for a word
___ 4. Finding an antonym for a word

5. In your own words, briefly explain the difference between a dictionary and thesaurus.

_____
_____
_____

#314. Using a Dictionary/Thesaurus 2

Use a **dictionary**. Circle the word in each group that is spelled correctly.

1. philosophy   phylosophy
   phylosophi   philosofy
2. languige   language
   lanugage   lanwage
3. liberry   libery
   libary   library
4. scientest   sighentist
   sciantist   scientist
5. aperatus   apparatus
   aperatis   aparatus

#315. Using a Dictionary/Thesaurus 3

Use a **thesaurus**. Write at least two **synonyms** for each word.

1. **appearance** _____
2. **say** _____
3. **freedom** _____
4. **look** _____

Use a **thesaurus** to find at least two **antonyms** for each word.

5. **success** _____
6. **moist** _____
7. **modern** _____
8. **independent** _____

#316. Using a Dictionary/Thesaurus 4

Look up each word in a **dictionary** and write a definition for each word.

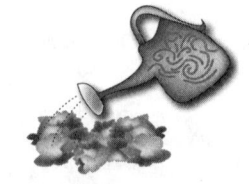

1. **postulate** _____
   _____
2. **hydrate** _____
   _____
3. **diatribe** _____
   _____
4. **peevish** _____
   _____
5. **brandish** _____
   _____

CD-404245 ©Mark Twain Media, Inc., Publishers

LANGUAGE ARTS WARM-UPS: Expanding Vocabulary   Answer Keys

Answer Keys

Teachers: Check students' work if necessary.

Root Words, Prefixes, and Suffixes

#001. Introduction to Root Words, Prefixes, and Suffixes 1 (p. 2)
Answers will vary. Possible answers include:
1. unbelievable   2. important   3. reprinted

#002. Introduction to Root Words, Prefixes, and Suffixes 2 (p. 2)
1. inaction, income, inform
2. disregard, disassemble
3. reaction, reassemble, repay, reform

#003. Introduction to Root Words, Prefixes, and Suffixes 3 (p. 2)
Semimonthly (or fortnightly, which also means every two weeks)

#004. Introduction to Root Words, Prefixes, and Suffixes 4 (p. 2)
Correct words: careful, fitted, regularly.
Corrections: tuning, swimming

#005. Introduction to Root Words, Prefixes, and Suffixes 5 (p. 3)
Answers will vary.

#006. Introduction to Root Words, Prefixes, and Suffixes 6 (p. 3)
Any sentence using comfort.

#007. Introduction to Root Words, Prefixes, and Suffixes 7 (p. 3)
relocate, located, locatable. Sentences will vary.

#008. Introduction to Root Words, Prefixes, and Suffixes 8 (p. 3)
Possible word to use: incomparable

#009. Root Words, Prefixes, and Suffixes 1 (p. 4)
Answers will vary.

#010. Root Words, Prefixes, and Suffixes 2 (p. 4)
Prefixes: anti-, dis-; *Root word*: establish; Suffixes: -ment, -arian, -ism
According to freedictionary.com, this word means "the doctrine or political position that opposes the withdrawal of state recognition of an established church, especially concerning the Anglican Church in England." [Note: It is not important that students actually learn and use this word, but it is a fun one to discuss.]

#011. Root Words, Prefixes, and Suffixes 3 (p. 4)
Antitoxin, antidote, and antiserum share similar meanings. Sentences will vary.

#012. Root Words, Prefixes, and Suffixes 4 (p. 4)
1. Answers will vary.
2. because the *re-* is part of the root word

#013. Root Words, Prefixes, and Suffixes 5 (p. 5)
1. think   2. legal   3. honest
4. manage   5. possible   6. connect

#014. Root Words, Prefixes, and Suffixes 6 (p. 5)
Answers will vary.

#015. Root Words, Prefixes, and Suffixes 7 (p. 5)
1. believe   2. happy   3. appear
4. friend   5. charge   6. agree

#016. Root Words, Prefixes, and Suffixes 8 (p. 5)
Sentences will vary.
1. remove   2. repay   3. replace
The prefix *re-* means to do again.

#017. Prefixes 1 (p. 6)
Deifinitions will vary.
1. unlikely   2. nonprofit   3. nonsense
4. untidy

#018. Prefixes 2 (p. 6)
Definitions will vary.
1. illogical   2. immature   3. inactive
4. illiterate   5. irregular

#019. Prefixes 3 (p. 6)
1. T   2. T   3. T   4. F

#020. Prefixes 4 (p. 6)
1. C   2. A   3. B   4. D

#021. Prefixes 5 (p. 7)
1. Answers will vary.
2. *Interstate* means "among two or more states"; *intrastate* means "within the same state."

#022. Prefixes 6 (p. 7)
Answers will vary. Some possible words are listed.
1. transfer; transmit; transport; transcend; transcript
2. international; interstate; intermediate; intercession; interim
3. subway; subnormal; subtract; subroutine; subscript; subterranean

CD-404245 ©Mark Twain Media, Inc., Publishers   81

Language Arts Warm-Ups: Expanding Vocabulary   **Answer Keys**

#023. Prefixes 7 (p. 7)
1. F 2. T 3. F 4. T 5. F

#024. Prefixes 8 (p. 7)
Answers will vary.

#025. Prefixes With Negative Meanings 1 (p. 8)
They all mean "no" or "not."

#026. Prefixes With Negative Meanings 2 (p. 8)
Definitions will vary.
1. unable 2. unlike 3. undo 4. unmade
5. uncover

#027. Prefixes With Negative Meanings 3 (p. 8)
1. disrepair 2. disarm 3. disorder
4. disloyal 5. disable 6. discolored
7. discharge 8. disrespect

#028. Prefixes With Negative Meanings 4 (p. 8)
Answers will vary.

#029. Prefixes With Negative Meanings 5 (p. 9)
Sentences will vary.
1. distrust 2. untrue 3. disobey
4. unbearable

#030. Prefixes With Negative Meanings 6 (p. 9)
1. unlimited; without end
2. wrong; incorrect; unsuitable
3. restless; anxious
4. unreasonable; senseless

#031. Prefixes With Negative Meanings 7 (p. 9)
unbend unbolt unborn unclog uneven
unfair unfed unfit unglue
unknown unmade unreal untied untrue
unused unusual

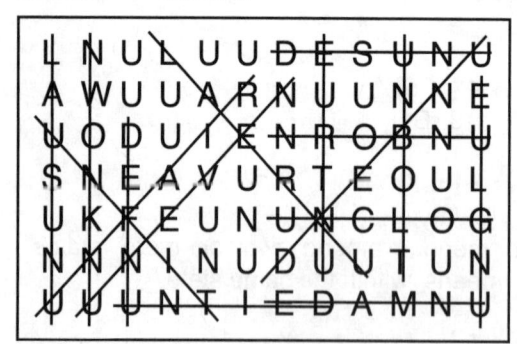

[word search grid]

#032. Prefixes With Negative Meanings 8 (p. 9)
1. B 2. A 3. A 4. B 5. B

#033. Prefixes With Negative Meanings 9 (p. 10)
Sentences will vary.
1. disadvantage 2. disapprove 3. disconnect
4. disprove

#034. Prefixes With Negative Meanings 10 (p. 10)
1. to not obey 2. Answers will vary. Any charity, etc.
3. not poisonous 4–5. Answers will vary.

#035. Prefixes With Negative Meanings 11 (p. 10)
1. E 2. D 3. F 4. B 5. A 6. C

#036. Prefixes With Negative Meanings 12 (p. 10)
1. The word is typed incorrectly.
2. The socks are not a pair; each one is different.
3. You could get lost.
4. Answers will vary. The student could be punished, etc.

#037. Prefixes Denoting Numbers 1 (p. 11)
Answers will vary.

#038. Prefixes Denoting Numbers 2 (p. 11)
1. hexagon 2. triceratops 3. octopus
4. centennial

#039. Prefixes Denoting Numbers 3 (p. 11)
1. decathlon 2. quadruplets 3. quintet
4. bimonthly

#040. Prefixes Denoting Numbers 4 (p. 11)
1. 10 2. meter 3. 1,000 4. meter
5. 100 6. 1,000

#041. Prefixes Denoting Numbers 5 (p. 12)
1. bilingual 2. pentathlon 3. bicentennial
4. trilogy 5. bisect 6. triplets 7. October

#042. Prefixes Denoting Numbers 6 (p. 12)
1. July 2. November, 2016 3. July, 2014
4. Once every 100 years 5. July 4, 2076

#043. Prefixes Denoting Numbers 7 (p. 12)
1. millipede 2. 1,000 3. 100
4. Each lens is divided into two parts.

#044. Prefixes Denoting Numbers 8 (p. 12)
1 uni- 2 bi- 3 tri- 4 quad- 5 penta- or quin
6 hex- 8 oct- 10 dec- 100 cent- 1,000 milli-

#045. Prefixes over- and under- 1 (p. 13)
1. A 2. B 3. B 4. C 5. C 6. A

#046. Prefixes over- and under- 2 (p. 13)
Answers will vary.

#047. Prefixes in-, im-, and ex- 1 (p. 13)
1. to breathe out 2. to leave out
3. to burst outward 4. out

Language Arts Warm-Ups: Expanding Vocabulary — Answer Keys

#048. Prefixes in-, im-, and ex-2 (p. 13)
1. To *incite* is to move to action or to urge on. To *excite* is to increase the activity of or stimulate.
2. *Import* is to bring something in. *Export* is to send something out.
3. *Expire* is to die, come to an end, or breathe one's last breath. *Inspire* is to motivate, affect, or breathe in.

#049. Prefixes Denoting Size and Position 1 (p. 14)
1–2. Answers will vary.
3. There are two people sharing the room.

#050. Prefixes Denoting Size and Position 2 (p. 14)
1. small
2. a small community seen as representing the epitome, or best, of a larger community
3. It enlarges images of tiny objects so they can be seen.

#051. Prefixes Denoting Size and Position 3 (p. 14)
1. EVA stands for extravehicular activity.
2. ESP stands for extrasensory perception.
3. ET stands for extraterrestrial.

#052. Prefixes Denoting Size and Position 4 (p. 14)
1. hyper- 2. hypo- 3. very loud 4. low

#053. Prefixes Denoting Size and Position 5 (p. 15)
1. A 2. C 3. A 4. A
5. B 6. A 7. A/B 8. A

#054. Prefixes Denoting Size and Position 6 (p. 15)
1. interchange 2. intermural 3. intramural
4. interstate 5. intrastate 6. intercontinental

#055. Prefixes Denoting Size and Position 7 (p. 15)
1. megabats
2. 1,048,576 bytes in a megabyte (Accept one million.)
3. Answers will vary.

#056. Prefixes Denoting Size and Position 8 (p. 15)
Definitions will vary. Possible answers are given.
1. to pass from a higher place to a lower one
2. to remove insects; to eliminate errors
3. to put off, postpone
4. to infer from a general principle
5. to slope downward; to become less
6. a quality that deserves blame or lacks merit
7. to take away from a total

#057. Prefix Review 1 (p. 16)
Answers will vary.

#058. Prefix Review 2 (p. 16)
1. pre- 2. macro- 3. mis- 4. micro-
5. re- 6. over- 7. hyper- 8. sub-

#059. Prefix Review 3 (p. 16)
Answers may vary. Possible answers are given.
1. deactivate 2. interstate, intrastate
3. deformed 4. extraordinary
5. depart 6. megaphone, microphone
7. deport, export
8. interactive, hyperactive, hypoactive

#060. Prefix Review 4 (p. 16)
1. *dis*agree 2. *dis*trust 3. *in*sincere
4. *in*correct 5. *in*direct 6. *im*mortal
7. *im*polite 8. *mis*fit 9. *mis*trust
10. *non*stop 11. *non*profit 12. *over*head
13. *over*heat 14. *over*weight 15. *un*happy
16. *un*selfish 17. *under*foot 18. *under*line
19. *re*place 20. *il*legal

#061. Prefix Review 5 (p. 17)
Answers will vary.

#062. Prefix Review 6 (p. 17)
Sentences will vary.
1. unfamiliar 2. informal 3. illegible
4. impractical 5. dissatisfied, unsatisfied
6. intolerable

#063. Prefix Review 7 (p. 17)
1. no 2. no 3. yes 4. yes 5. yes 6. no
7. no 8. yes 9. yes 10. no 11. no 12. no

#064. Prefix Review 8 (p. 17)
Definitions will vary. Possible answers are given.
1. To *miscalculate* is to calculate wrongly. To *recalculate* is to calculate again.
2. *Disorder* means out of order or in the wrong order. To *reorder* is to put back in order or to order something again.
3. *Bicentennial* is something that happens every 200 years. *Biannual* is something that happens twice a year.
4. *Removed* means that something has been moved or gotten rid of. *Unmoved* means that something has not been moved.
5. The *pentathlon* consists of five events. The *decathlon* consists of ten events

#065. Prefix Review 9 (p. 18)
Answers may vary. Some possible answers are listed.
1. disloyal 2. biannual 3. discolor, recolor
4. bicycle, unicycle, tricycle, recycle 5. hemisphere
6. undone, redone, overdone, underdone
7. misuse, reuse 8. rethink
9. repaint 10. replace, displace, misplace

#066. Prefix Review 10 (p. 18)
1. D 2. F 3. H 4. G 5. E 6. A 7. B
8. C

#067. Prefix Review 11 (p. 18)
1. macroorganisms 2. sell to 3. intracontinental
4. No 5. Answers will vary (any two planets).

#068. Prefix Review 12 (p. 18)
1. T 2. T 3. F 4. F 5. F 6. T 7. T

#069. Suffixes 1 (p. 19)
Definitions will vary.
1. homeless 2. awesome
3. senseless 4. fearsome; fearless

#070. Suffixes 2 (p. 19)
1. lovable 2. retirement 3. sensible

#071. Suffixes 3 (p. 19)
1. T 2. F 3. F

#072. Suffixes 4 (p. 19)
Sentences will vary.

#073. Suffixes 5 (p. 20)
Words will vary. Possible answers listed.
1. friendship; courtship 2. avoidance; compliance
3. outlandish; foolish

#074. Suffixes 6 (p. 20)
1. Answers will vary.
2. A *democracy* is a system where the people have freedom to elect officials. *Demographic* refers to the characteristics of a people in a given area.

#075. Suffixes 7 (p. 20)
1. (present) F 2. (select) D 3. (explore) B
4. (appreciate) E 5. (reflect) A 6. (elect) C

#076. Suffixes 8 (p. 20)
1. F 2. F 3. F 4. T 5. F

#077. Adding Suffixes 1 (p. 21)
Answers will vary.

#078. Adding Suffixes 2 (p. 21)
Answers will vary.

#079. Adding Suffixes 3 (p. 21)
The spelling of all words except slow, tall, direct, rapid, and short will change. Sentences will vary.

#080. Adding Suffixes 4 (p. 21)
1. adopt 2. agree 3. style 4. combine
5. day 6. decorate 7. direct 8. govern
9. invite 10. twitch

#081. Suffixes -er, -or, -est 1 (p. 22)
1. hotter 2. sadder 3. colder 4. tastier
5. funnier 6. redder 7. higher 8. dryer or drier

#082. Suffixes -er, -or, -est 2 (p. 22)
1. speediest 2. wisest 3. closest 4. jolliest
5. tiniest 6. wettest 7. freshest 8. oldest
9. spiciest 10. yes

#083. Suffixes -er, -or, -est 3 (p. 22)
1. baker 2. director 3. golfer 4. governor
5. jogger 6. singer 7. manager 8. writer

#084. Suffixes -er, -or, -est 4 (p. 22)
1. "one who" 2. Answers will vary.

#085. Suffixes -ly and -ful 1 (p. 23)
Sentences will vary. Adverb forms:
1. broadly 2. politely 3. quickly 4. quietly
5. rudely 6. sadly 7. shyly 8. silently
9. timidly 10. weakly

#086. Suffixes -ly and -ful 2 (p. 23)
1. "filled with" or "full of"
2–3. Answers will vary.

#087. Suffixes -ly and -ful 3 (p. 23)
Sentences will vary.
1. colorful 2. graceful 3. plentiful 4. playful

#088. Suffixes -ly and -ful 4 (p. 23)
1. F 2. H 3. I 4. G 5. J
6. B 7. E 8. C 9. A 10. D

#089. Suffixes -less, -tion, -ation 1 (p. 24)
1. *-less* means without or unable to act
2–6. Answers will vary.

#090. Suffixes -less, -tion, -ation 2 (p. 24)
Some answers will vary.
1. tasteful 2. graceful 3. careful 4. eternal
5. no errors 6. There were no horses pulling them.

Language Arts Warm-Ups: Expanding Vocabulary   Answer Keys

#091. Suffixes -less, -tion, -ation 3 (p. 24)
Definitions will vary. Noun forms are:
1. donation   2. admiration   3. regulation
4. cooperation   5. inspiration

#092. Suffixes -less, -tion, -ation 4 (p. 24)
1. G   2. B   3. H   4. E   5. D   6. C
7. A   8. F

#093. Suffixes -able and -ment 1 (p. 25)
1. avoidable   2. bearable   3. bendable
4. comparable   5. inflatable   6. likable
7. lovable   8. removable   9. respectable
10. usable   11. capable of, fit for, or worthy of

#094. Suffixes -able and -ment 2 (p. 25)
Answers will vary.

#095. Suffixes -able and -ment 3 (p. 25)
Definitions will vary.
1. adjustment   2. advertisement   3. amusement
4. assignment   5. excitement   6. judgment
7. management   8. payment
(Note: *judgment* is an exception to the spelling rule.)

#096. Suffixes -able and -ment 4 (p. 25)
Answers will vary.

#097. Suffixes -ology, -ist, -phobia 1 (p. 26)
1. life   2. animals   3. myths   4. the earth
5. people and cultures   6. the human mind
7. ancient artifacts and writings   8. fish

#098. Suffixes -ology, -ist, -phobia 2 (p. 26)
1. plants   2. flowers   3. teeth   4. harp
5. biologist

#099. Suffixes -ology, -ist, -phobia 3 (p. 26)
1. chemistry   2. bicycle, motorcycle, etc.   3. pianist
4. helps people overcome physical or mental problems through therapy
5. type   6. weather and climate

#100. Suffixes -ology, -ist, -phobia 4 (p. 26)
1. heights   2. bees   3. water   4. sunshine
5. fear

#101. Suffixes -ish, -ness, -an 1 (p. 27)
Definitions will vary.
1. babyish   2. bluish   3. childish
4. greenish   5. reddish   6. stylish

#102. Suffixes -ish, -ness, -an 2 (p. 27)
Definitions will vary.
1. dizziness   2. easiness   3. firmness
4. laziness   5. loneliness   6. meekness

#103. Suffixes -ish, -ness, -an 3 (p. 27)
1. Swedish   2. Australian   3. Turkish
4. Finnish   5. Romans

#104. Suffixes -ish, -ness, -an 4 (p. 27)
1. Spanish   2. Egyptian   3. Italian
4. Hawaiian (or some may be Polynesian)
5. Russian   6. Polish   7. Mexican
8. Irish

#105. Suffix Review 1 (p. 28)
1. yes: beautiful   2. yes: desirable   3. no
4. no   5. yes: happily   6. yes: iciest

#106. Suffix Review 2 (p. 28)

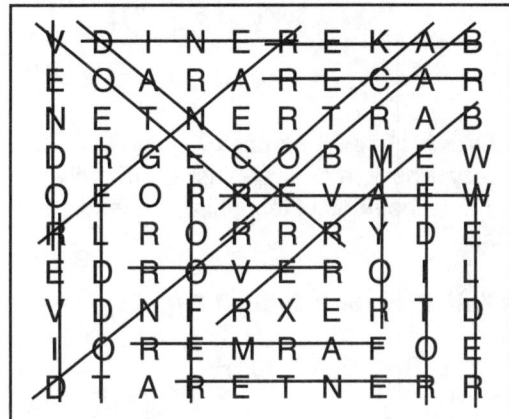

[word search puzzle]

#107. Suffix Review 3 (p. 28)
Answers will vary.

#108. Suffix Review 4 (p. 28)
1. T   2. T   3. T   4. F   5. F   6. T

#109. Suffix Review 5 (p. 29)
1. -ly   2. -able   3. -ish   4. -phobia
5. -ful   6. -less   7. -er   8. -ology

#110. Suffix Review 6 (p. 29)
Examples will vary.
1. noun   3. adjective   5. adjective

#111. Suffix Review 7 (p. 29)
Examples will vary.
1. adverb   3. noun   5. noun

#112. Suffix Review 8 (p. 29)
Answers will vary. Possible words include repay, prepay, payment, payable, paying, repayment, prepayment.

#113. Words With Prefixes & Suffixes 1 (p. 30)
Root words are listed:
1. direct   2. direct   3. invest   4. invest
5. observe   6. observe   7. observe
8. propose   9. propose   10. invest

Language Arts Warm-Ups: Expanding Vocabulary   Answer Keys

#114. Words With Prefixes & Suffixes 2 (p. 30)
Answers will vary.

#115. Words With Prefixes & Suffixes 3 (p. 30)
Answers will vary. Some possible answers are fulfill, refill, filling, filler, fulfillment, overfill, unfilled, and unfulfilled.

#116. Words With Prefixes & Suffixes 4 (p. 30)
1. B   2. B   3. B   4. A   5. B   6. B   7. A

#117. Words With Prefixes & Suffixes 5 (p. 31)
Answers will vary. Possible answers include chargeable, uncharged, overcharged, undercharged, recharged, discharge, and turbocharger.

#118. Words With Prefixes & Suffixes 6 (p. 31)
1. V/A   2. N   3. V   4. V   5. N
6. N   7. N   8. V   9. A   10. V

#119. Words With Prefixes & Suffixes 7 (p. 31)
Answers will vary. Possible answers include friendly, unfriendly, friendless, befriend, friendship, unfriendliness, and friendliness.

#120. Words With Prefixes & Suffixes 8 (p. 31)
1. F   2. T   3. F   4. T   5. T
6. T   7. F   8. T   9. T   10. F

#121. Words With Prefixes & Suffixes 9 (p. 32)
1. B   2. E   3. A   4. F   5. D   6. C

#122. Words With Prefixes & Suffixes 10 (p. 32)
1. (n.) the act of finding out
2. (n.) one who finds out or detects
3. (n.) one who detects or a device for detecting
4. (adj.) not able to be detected

#123. Words With Prefixes & Suffixes 11 (p. 32)
1. V   2. N   3. N   4. N   5. N
6. N   7. V   8. N   9. A   10. A

#124. Words With Prefixes & Suffixes 12 (p. 32)
Answers will vary. Possible answers include lovable, unloved, lovelier, lovely, loveliest, loving, lover, beloved, and loveless.

#125. Root Words, Prefixes, and Suffixes Review 1 (p. 33)
Answers will vary.

#126. Root Words, Prefixes, and Suffixes Review 2 (p. 33)
1. justice: fairness   2. daring: boldness
3. speed: quickness   4. rude: disrespectful
5. chaos: disorder   6. falling apart: disrepair

#127. Root Words, Prefixes, and Suffixes Review 3 (p. 33)
1. E   2. D   3. H   4. B
5. F   6. G   7. C   8. A

#128. Root Words, Prefixes, and Suffixes Review 4 (p. 33)
Answers will vary. Some possible answers are listed.
1. cover: uncover, recover, undercover, discover
2. lay: underlay, overlay, relay, delay
3. cooked: uncooked, overcooked, undercooked, pre-cooked

#129. Root Words, Prefixes, and Suffixes Review 5 (p. 34)
1. C   2. E   3. B   4. F   5. A   6. G   7. D

#130. Root Words, Prefixes, and Suffixes Review 6 (p. 34)
1. C   2. G   3. B   4. F
5. D   6. H   7. A   8. E

#131. Root Words, Prefixes, and Suffixes Review 7 (p. 34)
Answer may vary. Some possible answers are listed.
1. agree: agreeable, agreement, agreeing, agreeably
2. bold: boldly, bolder, boldest, boldness
3. like: likely, likeness, likeliness, likelihood, likable

#132. Root Words, Prefixes, and Suffixes Review 8 (p. 34)
1. misshapen   2. discharge   3. nonsense
4. misdeed   5. millennium   6. decorations
7. fanciful   8. bisect   9. observation

Compound Words

#133. Compound Words 1 (p. 35)
1. cup/board; card/board; tea/cups; table/spoons
2. red/head; out/standing; work/out; foot/ball
3. stock/room; how/ever; can/not; white/wash; stair/case; after/noon; paint/brush

#134. Compound Words 2 (p. 35)
1. a type of snake   2. excess; overflow
3. a measure of power in an engine
4. a key on a keyboard that allows the operator to move backwards one character at a time
5. exclusive rights   6. landing strip; walkway

#135. Compound Words 3 (p. 35)
1. water fall   2. waterfall   3. anybody
4. any body   5. overalls   6. over all

Language Arts Warm-Ups: Expanding Vocabulary　　　　　　　　　　　　　Answer Keys

#136. Compound Words 4 (p. 35)
Cross out turkey, frontier, and walrus.

#137. Compound Words 5 (p. 36)
1–3. water
4–5. Two of these: hotcake; pancake; flapjack

#138. Compound Words 6 (p. 36)
piggyback, pigpen, pigtail, pillowcase, pincushion, pineapple, pipeline, pitchfork, platform, playground, playpen, playwright, plywood, polecat, policeman, and more

#139. Compound Words 7 (p. 36)
A. handlebar　B. wheelbarrow　C. skateboard

#140. Compound Words 8 (p. 36)
1–2. Possible answers: *Where the Sidewalk Ends*; *Mister Seahorse*; *Rugrats*; *The Indian in the Cupboard*; *Peter and the Starcatchers*; *The Lord of the Rings: The Fellowship of the Ring*
3. Corrections: bookkeeper; newsroom; blueberry

#141. Compound Words 9 (p. 37)
1. whitewall　2. blacktop　3. blackbird
4. whitecap　5. whitefish/blackfish
6. blackberry　7. whitewash

#142. Compound Words 10 (p. 37)
forecast; foresee; foretell. Sentences will vary.

#143. Compound Words 11 (p. 37)
1. lifetime　2. anyplace　3. teenager

#144. Compound Words 12 (p. 37)
1–3. Answers will vary.　　　4–7. horse

#145. Compound Words 13 (p. 38)
1. bodyguard　2. headlight　3. spacewalk
4. paperback

#146. Compound Words 14 (p. 38)
1. Possible answers include: computer keyboard, typewriter keyboard, piano keyboard
2. Possible answers include: cookware, cupboards, dishcloth, dishwasher, high chair, saucepan, tablecloth, tabletop, tableware, teacup, teapot

#147. Compound Words 15 (p. 38)
courthouse, skyscraper, hometown, supermarket, ballroom, grandstand

#148. Compound Words 16 (p. 38)
Possible answers include:
1. ice　2. elementary, middle, or high　3. dots
4. tailback, tailcoat, tail end, tailgate, taillight, tailpiece, tailpipe, tailplane, tailspin, tailwind

#149. Compound Words 17 (p. 39)
1. software　2. butterscotch　3. waterproof
4. cartwheel　5. courtyard

#150. Compound Words 18 (p. 39)
1. sidewalk　2. drawbridge　3. carport or airport
4. flowerpot　5. drainpipe or stovepipe

#151. Compound Words 19 (p. 39)
Possible answers include:
1–3. toothbrush, firetruck, horsepower, and lunchroom
4–6. brainstorm, copyright, buttercup, and peppermint

#152. Compound Words 20 (p. 39)
1–3. Together and anywhere are correct. The others are tomorrow, because, and sometimes.
4–7. fish

#153. Compound Words 21 (p. 40)
1. sunrise　2. sunset　3. airplane　4. highway
5. Answers will vary.

#154. Compound Words 22 (p. 40)
Answers may vary.
1. The sun was shining so brightly, I wore my **sunglasses**. I wanted to **sunbathe**, so I put on my **sunscreen**. I wanted a **suntan**, but I didn't want a **sunburn** or **sunstroke**.
2. horseradish　3. honeydew　4. jelly bean
5. cornmeal

#155. Compound Words 23 (p. 40)
under: underdog, underground, undermine, underprice, underhand
super: supernatural, superpower, supermarket, supersonic

#156. Compound Words 24 (p. 40)
1–8. Possible answers include: backpack, campground, campsite, campfire, coffeepot, sleeping bag, suitcase, sweatshirt
9–12. Answers will vary.

#157. Compound Words 25 (p. 41)
1. Possible answer: George Clooney wrote the book's *foreword*.
2. Everyone　3. Every one

LANGUAGE ARTS WARM-UPS: Expanding Vocabulary — Answer Keys

#158. Compound Words 26 (p. 41)
Possible answers include: bookkeeper, housekeeper, peacekeeper, shopkeeper, timekeeper, zookeeper

#159. Compound Words 27 (p. 41)
1. stop 2. pin 3. neck 4. toe
5. book 6. dog 7. house 8. suit

#160. Compound Words 28 (p. 41)
1. bear 2. pig 3. terrier 4. rex 5. crab

#161. Compound Words 29 (p. 42)
1.–5. room

#162. Compound Words 30 (p. 42)
Answers will vary.

#163. Compound Words 31 (p. 42)
Possible answers include:
1. Hot Springs   2. Mammoth Caves
3. Grand Canyon, Grand Tetons, or Grand Forks
4. Rocky Mountains   5. Drawings will vary.

#164. Compound Words 32 (p. 42)
1. Answers will vary. 2. sun 3. moon 4. sun

#165. Compound Words 33 (p. 43)
1. Daughter-in-law, first-class, and age-old should be hyphenated.
2. Downtrodden, onetime, up-to-date, and sunbaked are adjectives. Cargo can also be used an an adjective.

#166. Compound Words 34 (p. 43)
1–3. Answers will vary. 4. foremost
5. seesaw or teeter-totter 6. springboard

#167. Compound Words 35 (p. 43)
1. raindrop 2. fishbowl 3. notebook

#168. Compound Words 36 (p. 43)
Correct compound words: sons-in-law, breakthroughs, backpack.
Shoestrings, starfishoo, and music boxes need to be corrected.

Vocabulary

#169. Confusing Word Pairs 1 (p. 44)
1. altogether 2. all together 3. all together
4. Altogether

#170. Confusing Word Pairs 2 (p. 44)
1. number 2. amount 3. amount
4. number

#171. Confusing Word Pairs 3 (p. 44)
1. between 2. among 3. among
4. between 5. between 6. among

#172. Confusing Word Pairs 4 (p. 44)
1. irritation 2. aggravated 3. irritated
4. continuous 5. continual

#173. Confusing Word Pairs 5 (p. 45)
Sentences will vary.
1. *borrow*: to receive something with the intention of returning the same or an equivalent
2. *loan*: money or an item received in exchange for a promise to pay it back, usually with interest
3. *fewer*: used with items or people that can be counted and is used with plural nouns
4. *less*: indicates amount or degree and is used with singular nouns

#174. Confusing Word Pairs 6 (p. 45)
1. affected 2. effect 3. except
4. accepted

#175. Confusing Word Pairs 7 (p. 45)
1. C 2. D 3. A 4. B

#176. Confusing Word Pairs 8 (p. 45)
1. well 2. good 3. good 4. well
5. good 6. well

#177. Homophones 1 (p. 46)
1. principles 2. principals 3. principal
4. principles

#178. Homophones 2 (p. 46)
1. D 2. B 3. F 4. A 5. C 6. E

#179. Homophones 3 (p. 46)
1. reigns; reins   2. straight; strait

#180. Homophones 4 (p. 46)
1. residence 2. pedal 3. peddle 4. residents

#181. Homophones 5 (p. 47)
Answers will vary. Some possible answers listed.
1. verb; quote
2. noun; a place
3. noun/verb; vision/to see
4. noun; a set of rooms in a motel or hotel
5. adjective; sugary

#182. Homophones 6 (p. 47)
1. C 2. F 3. A 4. E 5. D 6. B

Language Arts Warm-Ups: Expanding Vocabulary — Answer Keys

#183. Homophones 7 (p. 47)
1. horse; hoarse
2. lesson; lessen
3. patients; patience
4. teamed
5. beach; teemed

#184. Homophones 8 (p. 47)
1. altar – table; a raised table or platform used in worship or ritual
2. course – class; a number of lectures dealing with a subject of study

#185. Homographs 1 (p. 48)
1. to complete a course of instruction
2. a person who has completed a course of instruction
3. a flat surface
4. argued against

#186. Homographs 2 (p. 48)
1. lead   2. carries   3. behavior

#187. Homographs 3 (p. 48)
Definitions and sentences will vary.

#188. Homographs 4 (p. 48)
Definitions will vary.
1. ad´ / dress   2. ad / dress´   3. pre´ / sent
4. pre / sent´

#189. Synonyms 1 (p. 49)
1. cautious; prudent   2. minor
3. complex; difficult   4. enormous; mammoth
5. scrupulous; detailed; thorough

#190. Synonyms 2 (p. 49)
1. show   2. one   3. knight   4. illness   5. similar

#191. Synonyms 3 (p. 49)
Answers will vary. Possible answers are listed.
1. aggressive; warlike   2. lucky; favorable
3. power; influence   4. relic; ancient
5. exceptional; distinctive

#192. Synonyms 4 (p. 49)
Answers and definitions will vary. Possible answers are listed.
1. box; container   2. noise; loudness
3. understanding

#193. Antonyms 1 (p. 50)
1. B   2. C   3. D   4. E   5. A

#194. Antonyms 2 (p. 50)
Definitions will vary.
1. unreasonable   2. barely
3. ascent; climb   4. inadequate

#195. Antonyms 3 (p. 50)
1. scarce   2. lovable; sweet   3. ignore
4. ugliness   5. normal

#196. Antonyms 4 (p. 50)
Answers will vary. Possible answers are listed.
1. decelerate; brake   2. hesitant; unsure
3. land; sky   4. belittle; revile

#197. Proper Nouns and Proper Adjectives 1 (p. 51)
1. Czechoslovakian (Czech)   2. Ukrainian
3. Dutch   4. Greek   5. Azerbaijani (Azeri)
6. Finnish

#198. Proper Nouns and Proper Adjectives 2 (p. 51)
1. Hungarians   2. Lithuanians
3. Mozambicans   4. Zimbabweans

#199. Proper Nouns and Proper Adjectives 3 (p. 51)
1. Oklahoma   2. Minnesota   3. Massachusetts
4. Connecticut   5. Mississippi   6. Egypt
7. Afghanistan   8. Bangladesh   9. Lebanon
10. Malaysia   11. Kuwait

#200. Proper Nouns and Proper Adjectives 4 (p. 51)
Answers will vary. Check for correct spelling and capitalization.

#201. Changing the Part of Speech of Words 1 (p. 52)
1. beautiful   2. foolish   3. personal
4. national   5. stylish   6. musical

#202. Changing the Part of Speech of Words 2 (p. 52)
1. foolishly   2. childishly   3. additionally
4. fractionally   5. truthfully   6. wholly

#203. Changing the Part of Speech of Words 3 (p. 52)
1. complication   2. collision
3. computer; computation   4. official
5. confidence   6. patron

#204. Changing the Part of Speech of Words 4 (p. 52)
1. permanently   2. obviously   3. gradually
4. secondly   5. practically   6. medically
7. Answers will vary.

#205. Words From Mythology 1 (p. 53)
1. sphinx   2. centaur   3. mermaid   4. minotaur

#206. Words From Mythology 2 (p. 53)
1. D   2. C   3. A   4. B

Language Arts Warm-Ups: Expanding Vocabulary   Answer Keys

#207. Words From Mythology 3 (p. 53)
1. lion, goat, and serpent/snake   2. fly
3. The old phoenix was consumed by flames, and the new bird was reborn from the ashes.
4. Arabia   5. jinni, djinni

#208. Words From Mythology 4 (p. 53)
1. Ireland   2. Egypt   3. India
4. Someone in the house would die.   5. ☥

#209. Classifying Words 1 (p. 54)
These words are mammals: armadillo; echidna; javalina; narwhal; ocelot; pangolin

#210. Classifying Words 2 (p. 54)
These words are not documents: honorarium; jurisdiction; sinecure; tenure

#211. Classifying Words 3 (p. 54)
Fish: flounder; halibut; manta ray
Insects: cicada; earwig; praying mantis; walking stick; water strider
Amphibians: hellbender; mud puppy; newt; salamander; yellow-striped caecilian

#212. Classifying Words 4 (p. 54)
1. W   2. L   3. L   4. W   5. W
6. L   7. W   8. W   9. W   10. L

#213. Classifying Words 5 (p. 55)
1. B   2. D   3. C   4. A   5. E

#214. Classifying Words 6 (p. 55)
These words are not birds: barracuda; fibula; marlin; yellow jacket

#215. Classifying Words 7 (p. 55)
1. F   2. C   3. E   4. B   5. D   6. A

#216. Classifying Words 8 (p. 55)
1. the pound sign (#)
2. the sign (√) that means to find the square root
3. the number one followed by 100 zeros
4. a six-pointed star
5. a three-dimensional figure with eight triangular faces
6. an instrument used to measure angles

#217. Foreign Words and Phrases 1 (p. 56)
1. forbidden; prohibited
2. cabbage that has been pickled by soaking in a brine solution
3. a ghostly double or counterpart of a living person
4. a school for young children
5. used to wish someone good health, especially someone who has just sneezed

#218. Foreign Words and Phrases 2 (p. 56)
1. E   2. C   3. B   4. D   5. A

#219. Foreign Words and Phrases 3 (p. 56)
Sentences will vary.
1. hand to hand; one on one in a confrontation or conflict
2. sweet life; the good life
3. the common people

#220. Foreign Words and Phrases 4 (p. 56)
1. B   2. D   3. A   4. F   5. E   6. C

#221. Foreign Words and Phrases 5 (p. 57)
1. *chronicle:* a story or report told in the order in which events occurred
2. *chronic:* lasting for a long time; forever
3. *chronograph:* a stopwatch
4. *synchronize:* to set watches or clocks to exactly the same time

#222. Foreign Words and Phrases 6 (p. 57)
Sentences will vary.

#223. Latin Phrases 1 (p. 57)
Answers will vary. Possible answers are listed.
1. portable; comport; deport; export; import; report; support; transport
2. describe; description; prescribe; prescription; scribble; scriptures; subscribe; subscription; transcribe; transcription
3. eject; inject; interject; project; reject; subject
4. convert; divert; invert; revert; subvert

#224. Latin Phrases 2 (p. 57)
1. C   2. D   3. A   4. E   5. B

#225. Latin Phrases 3 (p. 58)
Sentences will vary.

#226. Latin Phrases 4 (p. 58)
1. Nothing; *pro bono* means "for the good" or "free of charge."
2. Probably not. It means "an unacceptable or unwelcome person."
3. They were sailing into "unknown territory"; places that had not been mapped.

#227. Latin Phrases 5 (p. 58)
Sentences will vary.
1. It is my fault.
2. Something in exchange for something of equal value
3. I came; I saw; I conquered.

LANGUAGE ARTS Warm-Ups: Expanding Vocabulary   Answer Keys

#228. Latin Phrases 6 (p. 58)
1. *in loco parentis*: in the place of a parent
2. *in medias res*: in the middle of something
3. *in situ*: situated in the original place

Figurative Language

#229. Idioms 1 (p. 59)
1. goes against my grain   2. on cloud nine
3. was all thumbs   4. cut the mustard

#230. Idioms 2 (p. 59)
1. I'm going to bed.
2. One picture should show cats and dogs falling from the sky, the other should show a rain downpour.

#231. Idioms 3 (p. 59)
1. Tanya was so nervous that her stomach felt fluttery.
2. burn the midnight oil

#232. Idioms 4 (p. 59)
2. got up on the wrong side of the bed
4. has a bee in her bonnet
5. had his dander up

#233. Idioms 5 (p. 60)
1. are the boss.   2. ask what's wrong.

#234. Idioms 6 (p. 60)
1. anything is possible; unlimited   2. very confusing
3. work until late at night; work long hours

#235. Idioms 7 (p. 60)
1. D   2. A   3. E   4. C   5. B

#236. Idioms 8 (p. 60)
Answers will vary.
1. reveal a secret; say something wrong
2. hard work   3. hurry
4. make a good impression
5. attempting something too difficult or dangerous

#237. Imagery 1 (p. 61)
Answers will vary.

#238. Imagery 2 (p. 61)
Answers will vary.

#239. Imagery 3 (p. 61)
Underline: buzzed, dark, smell, scent, sizzling, watered, growled, crunchy, cold, hard, soft, red

#240. Imagery 4 (p. 61)
1. scratchy; A. wool sweater   2. nubby; D. carpet
3. silky; B. angora fur   4. rough; E. sandpaper
5. soft; C. pillow

#241. Imagery 5 (p. 62)
Answers will vary.

#242. Imagery 6 (p. 62)
Answers will vary.

#243. Imagery 7 (p. 62)
1. basketball, cottonwood
2. The first mug has a flower design. The second mug has a chip on the rim. The third mug has a checked design.

#244. Imagery 8 (p. 62)
Answers will vary.

#245. Imagery 9 (p. 63)
Answers will vary.

#246. Imagery 10 (p. 63)
1. cry, bark, thud, tap, clomp, clap, whimper
2. smooth, rough, hard, sharp, crusty, sticky

#247. Imagery 11 (p. 63)
Answers will vary but may include: beep, boom, pop, pow, thud, thunk, whiz, vroom

#248. Imagery 12 (p. 63)
1. spicy, sweet, peppery, sour, bland, fruity
2. Answers will vary.

#249. Simile 1 (p. 64)
1. A girl is being compared to a hyena.
2. Answers will vary.

#250. Simile 2 (p. 64)
1. Love is like a rose.
2. Answers will vary, but should be something about March beginning with fierce weather and ending with mild weather.
3. Answers will vary.

#251. Simile 3 (p. 64)
1. My dog smells like gym socks.   2. Answers will vary.

#252. Simile 4 (p. 64)
Answers will vary.

#253. Simile 5 (p. 65)
Answers will vary.

Language Arts Warm-Ups: Expanding Vocabulary   Answer Keys

#254. Simile 6 (p. 65)
1. Sly as; C. a fox   2. Quiet as; D. a mouse
3. Gentle as; A. a lamb   4. Wise as; B. an owl

#255. Simile 7 (p. 65)
Answers will vary.

#256. Simile 8 (p. 65)
1. A rainbow is like a box of crayons.
2. Answers will vary.

#257. Metaphor 1 (p. 66)
1. Love is a rose.
2. Homework is being compared to an avalanche. It means that I have too much homework to be able to go to the movie.

#258. Metaphor 2 (p. 66)
Answers will vary.

#259. Metaphor 3 (p. 66)
1. Your thinking is compared to a train that has gone off the track.; your thinking has a problem.
2. No. Ann is special because it's her birthday.

#260. Metaphor 4 (p. 66)
1. Steven is being compared to a snake.
2. Answers will vary.

#261. Metaphor 5 (p. 67)
Answers will vary.

#262. Metaphor 6 (p. 67)
Answers will vary, but may mention that the metaphor is more direct and, therefore, more powerful.

#263. Metaphor 7 (p. 67)
Answers will vary.

#264. Metaphor 8 (p. 67)
1. My classroom is hot.   2. Answers will vary.

#265. Adage 1 (p. 68)
Answers will vary, but should say something about leaving things alone or not stirring up trouble.

#266. Adage 2 (p. 68)
1. Be good to those who provide for you.
2. "Don't cut off your nose to spite your face" and "Don't kill the goose that laid the golden egg" are similar in meaning.

#267. Adage 3 (p. 68)
1. rings   2. Answers will vary.

#268. Adage 4 (p. 68)
1. No pain, no gain.
2. Sometimes you have to take a risk to get a reward.

#269. Adage 5 (p. 69)
1. A picture is worth a thousand words.   2. play.

#270. Adage 6 (p. 69)
Answers will vary.

#271. Adage 7 (p. 69)
1. Answers will vary.
2. Answers will vary, but should say something about what you think you can do affects how successful you are.

#272. Adage 8 (p. 69)
People always think someone else is better off than they are. Answers will vary.

#273. Cliché 1 (p. 70)
1. mule   2. Answers will vary.

#274. Cliché 2 (p. 70)
Answers will vary.

#275. Cliché 3 (p. 70)
1. Answers will vary, but should mean that one is out of place in one's surroundings.
2. Answers will vary.

#276. Cliché 4 (p. 70)
1. Yes, it means the friend slept well.
2. Answers will vary.

#277. Cliché 5 (p. 71)
Answers will vary.

#278. Cliché 6 (p. 71)
1. Answers will vary.
2. The speed of light is 299,792,458 meters per second, or 186,282 miles per second (<www.ask.com>) According to the book, *It's Raining Frogs and Fishes*, by Jerry Dennis, lightning bolts travel at speeds up to 93,000 miles per second.

#279. Cliché 7 (p. 71)
Answers will vary.

#280. Cliché 8 (p. 71)
1. Answers will vary.
2. Answers will vary, but could include embarrassment, anger, and sunburn.

Language Arts Warm-Ups: Expanding Vocabulary Answer Keys

#281. Personificiation 1 (p. 72)
1. the truck   2. coughed   3. sputtered

#282. Personificiation 2 (p. 72)
Sentences will vary.
1. smiled   2. cruel

#283. Personificiation 3 (p. 72)
Sentences will vary.
1. winked   2. danced

#284. Personificiation 4 (p. 72)
1. The ocean waved goodbye.   2. Answers will vary.

#285. Personificiation 5 (p. 73)
Answers will vary.

#286. Personificiation 6 (p. 73)
Answers will vary.

#287. Personificiation 7 (p. 73)
The cactus brings us blooms in the spring.

#288. Personificiation 8 (p. 73)
Answers will vary.

#289. Allusion 1 (p. 74)
1. Winnie-the-Pooh. Answers will vary, but should indicate that Michael is a pessimist; he always thinks the worst will happen.
2. The Wizard of Oz

#290. Allusion 2 (p. 74)
1. Answers will vary, but should indicate that she entered without permission.
2. Answers will vary, but should indicate that Dr. Seuss' The Cat in the Hat made a big mess, left, and got the children into trouble.

#291. Allusion 3 (p. 74)
1. She is a detective.   2. He acts like a boy.

#292. Allusion 4 (p. 74)
1. long.
2. Someone from a lowly background becomes highly successful.

#293. Allusion 5 (p. 75)
1. Answers will vary, but should indicate that the person needs a heart.
2. Smokey Bear, whose motto is "Only you can prevent forest fires."

#294. Allusion 6 (p. 75)
1. he gets into everything.   2. the Ugly Duckling.

#295. Symbolism 1 (p. 75)
1. Answers will vary.   2. old age

#296. Symbolism 2 (p. 75)
1. owl   2. a diploma

#297. Symbolism 3 (p. 76)
1. hawk   2. dove

#298. Symbolism 4 (p. 76)
1. green   2. sadness.

#299. Symbolism 5 (p. 76)
1. a road   2. eternity

#300. Symbolism 6 (p. 76)
Answers will vary.

#301. Hyperbole 1 (p. 77)
1. a million   2. dull

#302. Hyperbole 2 (p. 77)
Answers will vary.

#303. Hyperbole 3 (p. 77)
Answers will vary.

#304. Hyperbole 4 (p. 77)
1. Answers will vary.
2. Answers will vary, but should indicate that a gunshot could really be heard for only a short distance.
3. Answers will vary, but should indicate that time cannot stand still.

#305. Hyperbole 5 (p. 78)
1. His eyes gave a violent look.   2. strong.

#306. Hyperbole 6 (p. 78)
1. boring   2. hot

#307. Hyperbole 7 (p. 78)
1. If I've told you once, C. I've told you a thousand times.
2. These math problems are so hard, A. even Einstein couldn't do them.
3 I want to win the game so bad, D. I can taste it.
4. She's so mean, B. she even makes Cruella De Vil look good.

#308. Hyperbole 8 (p. 78)
Answers will vary.

#309. Synecdoche 1 (p. 79)
1. car   2. king or queen

CD-404245 ©Mark Twain Media, Inc., Publishers 93

#310. Synecdoche 2 (p. 79)
1. workers
2. "Thank you." Threads means "clothing."

#311. Synecdoche 3 (p. 79)
1. the police officer   2. cattle.

#312. Synecdoche 4 (p. 79)
1. dinner.   2. the stage.

Dictionary Skills

#313. Using a Dictionary/Thesaurus 1 (p. 80)
1. D   2. T   3. D   4. T   5. Answers will vary.

#314. Using a Dictionary/Thesaurus 2 (p. 80)
1. philosophy   2. language   3. library
4. scientist   5. apparatus

#315. Using a Dictionary/Thesaurus 3 (p. 80)
Answers will vary. Possible answers are listed.
1. sight; show; scene; view; outlook
2. speak; utter; talk; state; declare
3. liberty; autonomy; independence; choice
4. see; stare; gaze; glance; spy
5. failure; malfunction; collapse
6. dry; arid; parched
7. antique; old-fashioned; traditional
8. dependent; needy, reliant

#316. Using a Dictionary/Thesaurus 4 (p. 80)
1. *postulate*: to assume or suggest something is true
2. *hydrate*: to provide water in order to maintain a correct fluid balance
3. *diatribe*: a criticism, often bitter or accusing in nature
4. *peevish*: fretful, cross, or complaining
5. *brandish*: to wave something about, often in a threatening manner

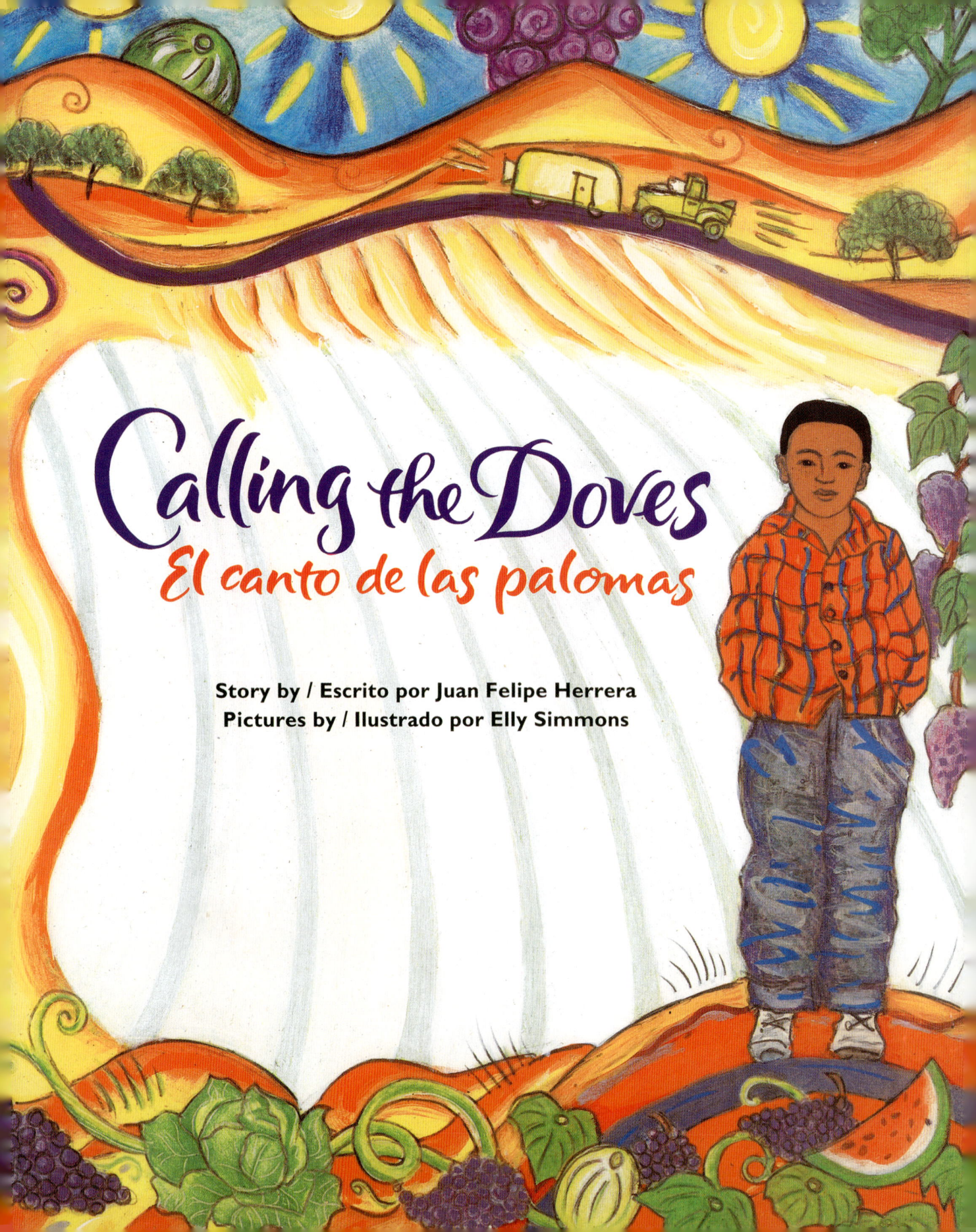

Calling the Doves
El canto de las palomas

Story by / Escrito por Juan Felipe Herrera
Pictures by / Ilustrado por Elly Simmons

Dedicated to the memory of Cesar Chavez and in honor of the work of the United Farmworkers Union. For John and Maralisa with love.
— *Elly Simmons*

El canto de las palomas by Felipe Herrera, illustrated by Elly Simmons. Text copyright © 1995 by Juan Felipe Herrera. Illustrations copyright © 1995 by Elly Simmons. Reprinted by permission of Children's Book Press.

Copyright © by Houghton Mifflin Harcourt Publishing Company

All rights reserved. No part of this work may be reproduced or transmitted in any form or by any means, electronic or mechanical, including photocopying or recording, or by any information storage and retrieval system, without the prior written permission of the copyright owner unless such copying is expressly permitted by federal copyright law. Requests for permission to make copies of any part of the work should be addressed to Houghton Mifflin Harcourt School Publishers, Attn: Permissions, 6277 Sea Harbor Drive, Orlando, Florida 32887-6777.

Printed in China

ISBN 10: 0-15-385937-7
ISBN 13: 978-0-15-385937-3

If you have received these materials as examination copies free of charge, Houghton Mifflin Harcourt School Publishers retains title to the materials and they may not be resold. Resale of examination copies is strictly prohibited.

Possession of this publication in print format does not entitle users to convert this publication, or any portion of it, into electronic format.

3 4 5 6 7 8 9 10   0940   18 17 16 15 14 13
4500441636

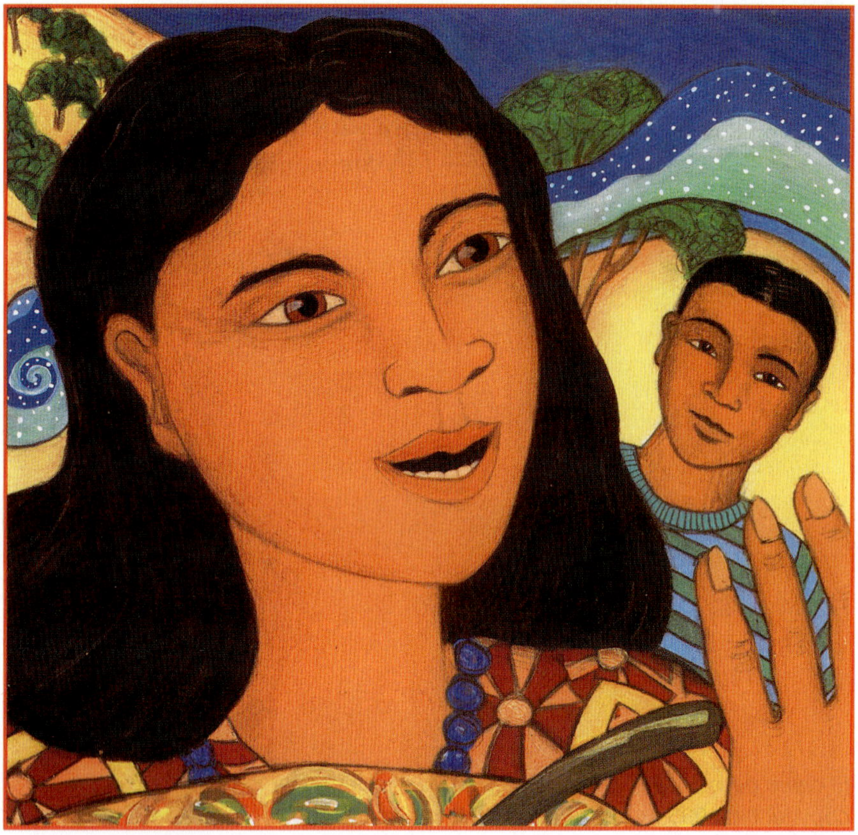

Nací en el pequeño pueblo de Fowler—
"la capital de las pasas del mundo".
Mi mamá y mi papá fueron campesinos
y yo crecí recorriendo con ellos
las montañas y los valles de California.

Dedico este librito a mi madre Lucha
y a mi padre Felipe, quienes amaban el cielo del campo
y la tierra cuando se pone tierna.
Ellos me enseñaron que dentro de cada palabra
existe una sonrisa.

"Naciste en el camino, como tu papá".

Mi mamá me decía esto
cuando teníamos que mudarnos a otro campo de labor.

Mi mamá Lucha, mi papá Felipe y yo.

Divisaba a los campesinos trabajando en los files
mientras mi papá manejaba nuestra vieja troca del Army
por los caminos olvidados de California.

Con su ropa brillante, los campesinos le daban color
al campo como aves tropicales.

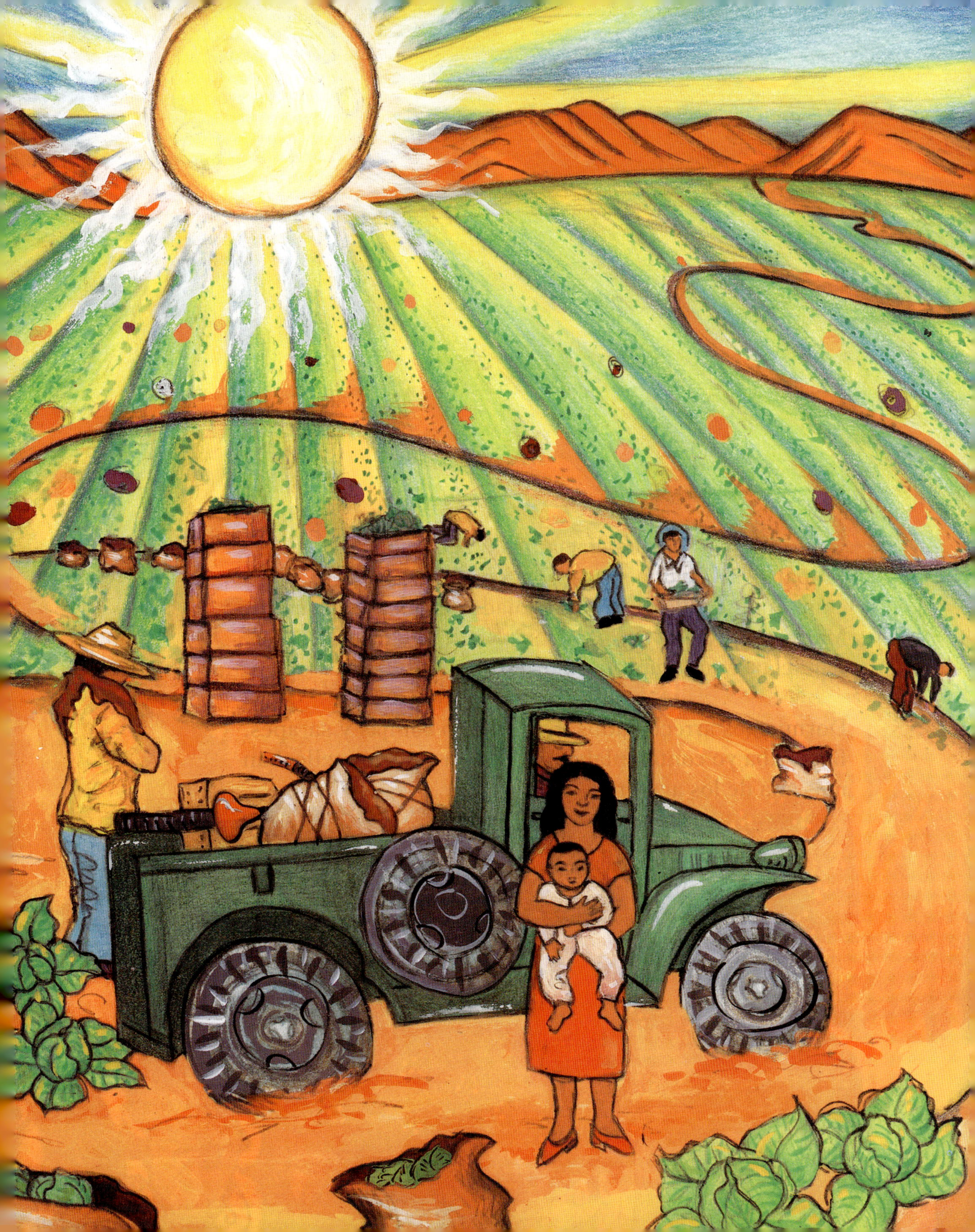

Mi mamá cocinaba el desayuno al aire libre.
Huevos con papas o huevos revueltos.

Una sartén, un comal para las tortillas
y un frasco con tenedores y cuchillos—
éstas eran las cosas necesarias.
Y, claro, leña para el fuego.

El cielo era mi cuchara azul
y el barro tierno de la tierra era mi plato.

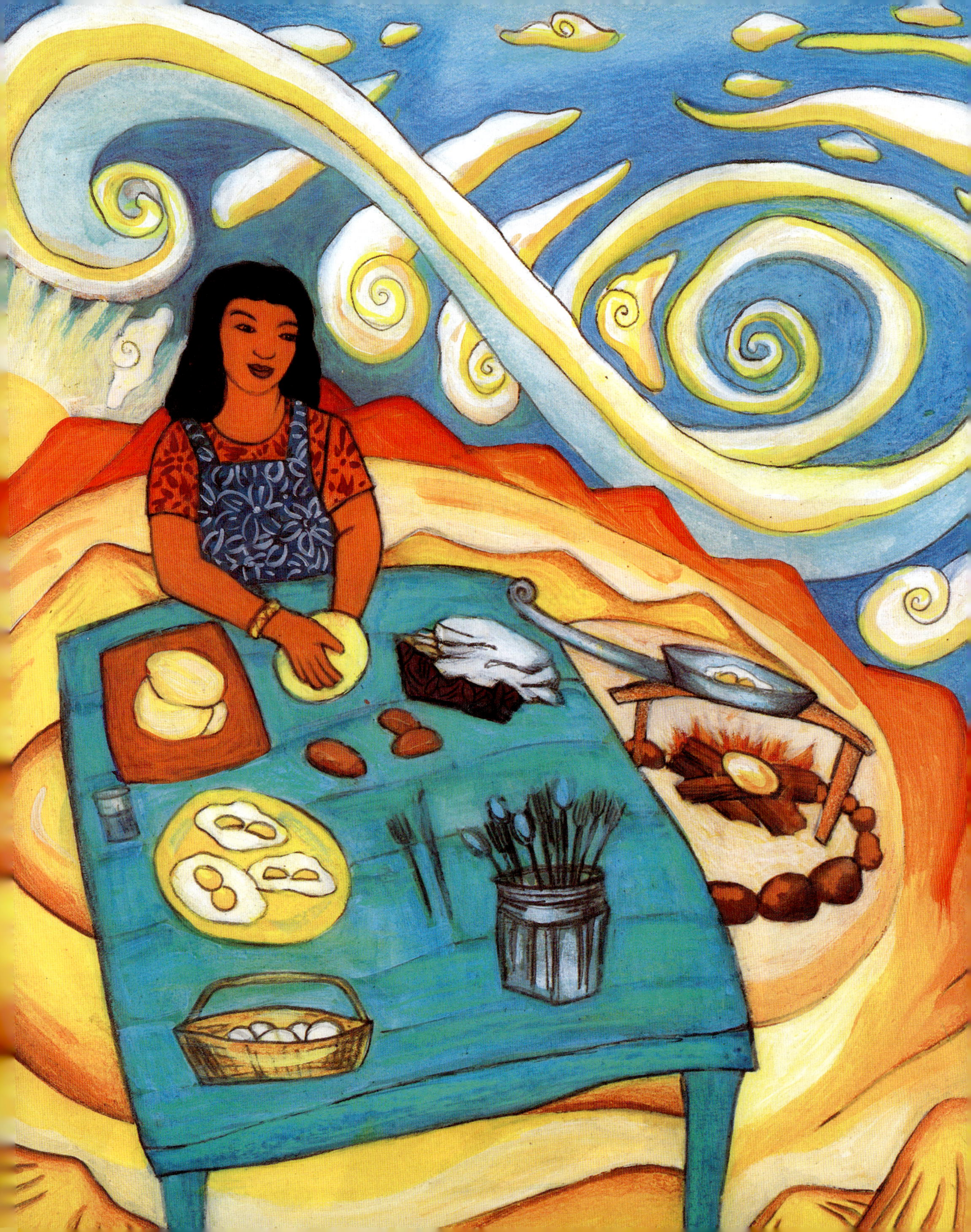

Un día mi papá decidió hacer
una casita de cuatro paredes
montada sobre un carro abandonado.
Martilló palos largos y madera laminada
sobre el chasis de un Ford antiguo y remojó
su brocha en baldes de pintura blanca.

Desde lejos, mi casa era
una caja chica de pan con ruedas.
Por dentro era una cuevita cariñosa
que se calentaba con pláticas.
Del radio en la pared salían
anuncios ruidosos y corridos mexicanos.

Adiós mi chaparrita, ya se va tu Pancho, muy lejos de tu rancho...

"Juan Felipe, ¿por qué tú no estás durmien[do]...

"¡Pero, Mamá!"

Una vez visitamos a unos amigos en Fowler por un par de meses.
Tomé mis baños en una tina de hojalata en medio del patio
rodeada por cuatro familias en sus casas rodantes.

Mientras me tallaba los brazos,
mi mamá cantaba de los mexicanos que cruzaban la frontera de Texas.
Yo seguía la canción y salpicaba el agua. Una iglesia protestante
hecha de madera frágil se ladeaba detrás de las casas rodantes.

Nuestro patio de barro
era un teatro vestido de arena
donde aprendí a cantar.

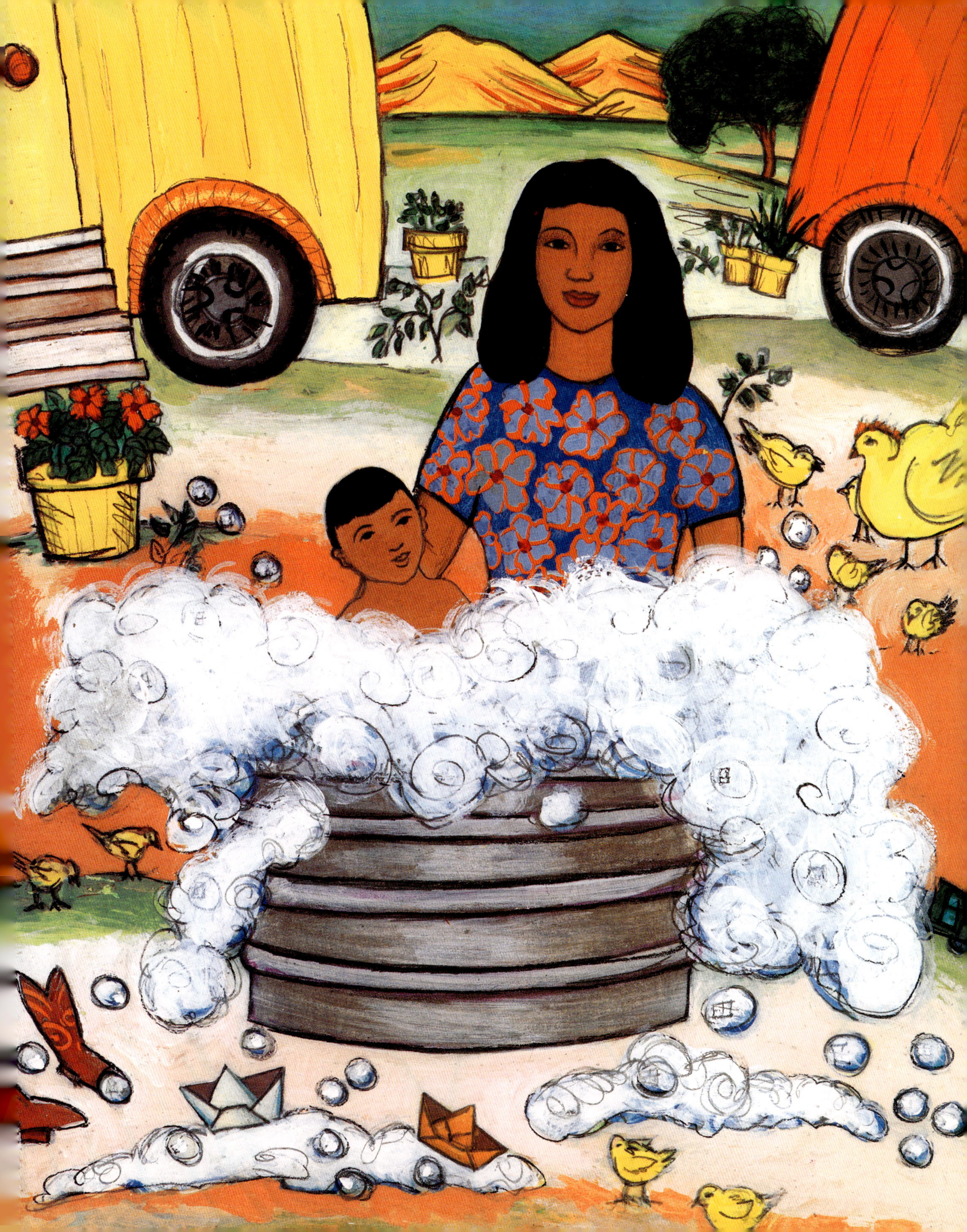

De vez en cuando mi madre nos sorprendía en la cena
recitando poesía.

Mientras cenábamos un platillo de guisado y una tortilla dura
de harina, se paraba de puntillas, con las manos levantadas,
como si pidiera lluvia a las nubes.

De sus labios brotaban palabras melodiosas
y por un momento el mundo entero dejaba de girar.

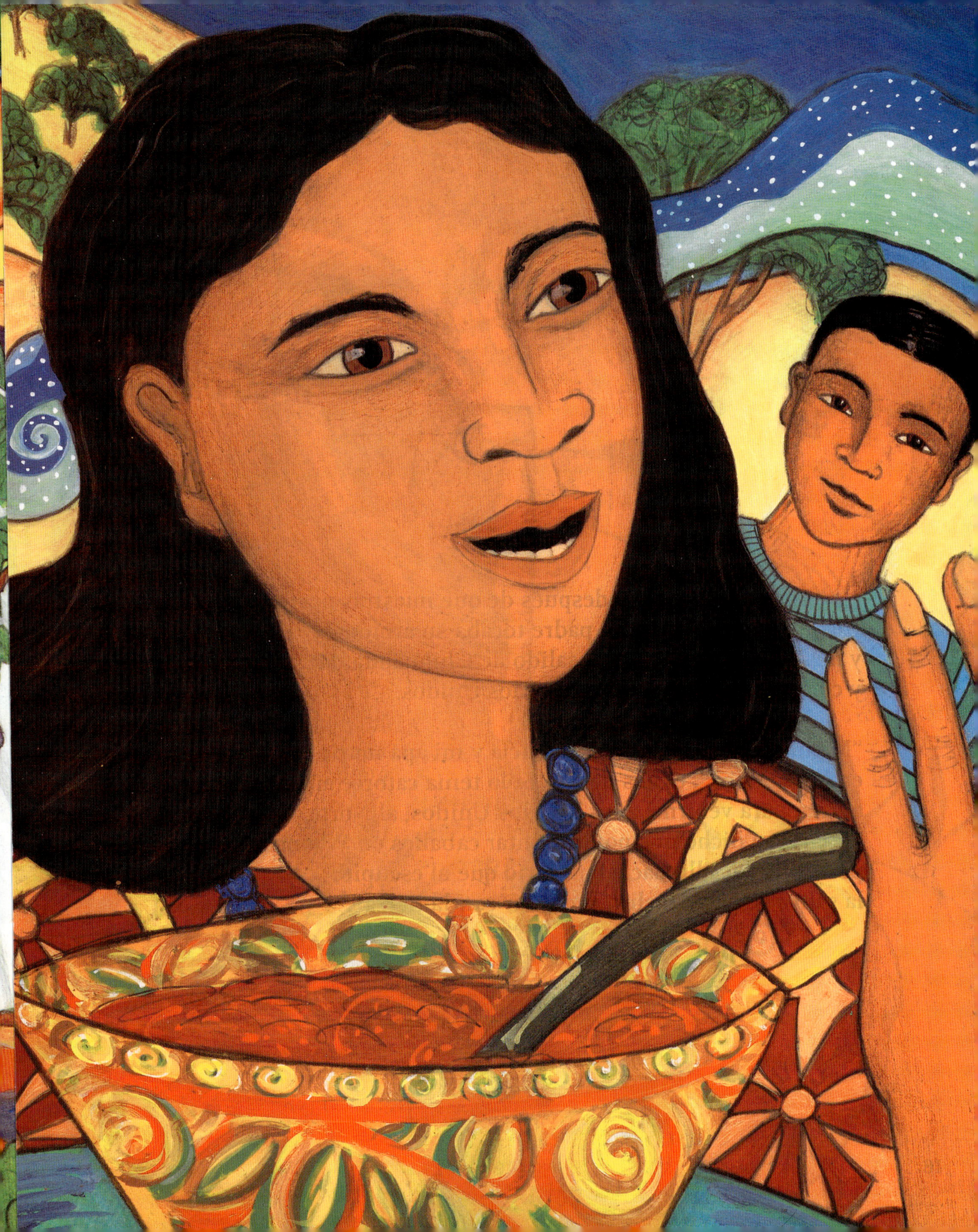

"Ya es tiempo de asentarnos. Es hora que Juanito
vaya a la escuela", al fin le dijo mi mamá a mi papá.

Tenía ocho años y ya había recogido los paisajes
del valle cerca de mi corazón:
con su tractor, mi papá le daba vueltas a la tierra,
con sus canciones, mi mamá levantaba su cara al sol.

Nuestra casita rodante bajaba en espiral
de las montañas hacia las ciudades del Sur de California.

Cuando las ciudades estaban a la vista, sabía
que algún día iba a seguir mi propio camino.
Mi voz volaría como los poemas que recitaba mi madre,
como el canto de las palomas que me enseñó mi padre.

JUAN FELIPE HERRERA is one of the most prominent Mexican American poets writing today. The award-winning author of five books of poetry, he is also an actor, a musician, and a popular professor at California State University at Fresno. He lives with his family in Fresno, California.

ELLY SIMMONS is an internationally-exhibited painter. Her first picture book for Children's Book Press, *Magic Dogs of the Volcanoes* by Manlio Argueto, was highly praised for its rich colors and magnificent imagery. She lives with her family in Lagunitas, California.